Praise for
Do I Need a Therapist?

"Finally! A critical missing link in the healing journey has been restored! This important book is absolutely essential for anyone looking for professional support and how to make the most out of it. Dr. Simon offers what we all need: lessons in how to be a savvy, engaged client who can make the most out of our experience of support and maximize our potential for lasting change."

Jonathan Ellerby, PhD,
bestselling author of *Inspiration Deficit Disorder: The No-Pill Prescription to End High Stress, Low Energy, and Bad Habits*

"Dr. Simon's book unveils all the myths about therapy. She has brought clarity to the field by explaining various types of therapies, who needs therapies, and how to strengthen therapist-patient relationships. This book is the road map for seeking therapy! Happy reading!"

Dr. Ben Louie,
**Certified Training & Development Professional,
Certified Performance Consultant**

"Jenny brings great wisdom and caring to her new book. It's like talking with a trusted friend."

**Chip McAuley, PhD,
Consciousness Theorist**

"One of the most vulnerable times in a person's life is when a life event knocks the wind out their sails and a person might feel lost or unable to process overwhelming emotions. Dr. Simon's new book, Do I Need a Therapist? A Consumer's Guide to Navigating Mental Health Services, *dives deep into what therapy is and what it is not. With two decades of experience in the field, Dr. Simon gives the reader an insider's view of the different kinds of therapy available and how to navigate the system successfully. This book should be a starting point for every person that is considering signing up for therapy. Highly recommended!"*

American Book Fest

"Therapy is not for everyone, but if you are seeking help, this book should be your first stop as it provides an excellent view into the counseling field. Dr. Simon's expertise and passion for honest dialogue surrounding a complicated topic brings much needed clarity and direction. This is a fantastic resource for anyone who desires a solid foundation when beginning the mental health journey."

**Dr. Scott A. Myers,
Higher Education Professional**

Do I Need a Therapist?

A CONSUMER'S GUIDE TO NAVIGATING MENTAL HEALTH SERVICES

Jenny Simon, PhD

Robert, Thank you for giving me hope and inspiration! I deeply appreciate you! Jenny

Copyright © 2019 by Jenny Simon

All rights reserved. This book or any portion thereof may not be reproduced or used in any manner whatsoever without the express written permission of the author except for the use of brief quotations in a book review.

Published in the United States of America

First printing, 2019
Editor: Nina Shoroplova
Book Formatting by Amit Dey | amitdey2528@gmail.com

Contact Information:
Rethinking Therapy
P.O. Box 32615
Tucson, AZ 85750
www.rethinkingtherapy.com

An important note: Although I am a licensed therapist, I am not *your* therapist. Reading this book does not create a client-therapist relationship. This book is not a substitute for an in-person mental health assessment by someone who is authorized in your state. Please check with your state regarding the specific licensure rules for behavioral health. This content is not intended to be a substitute for professional advice, diagnosis, or treatment. This author is not liable for any damages or negative consequences from any treatment, action, application, or preparation to any person reading or following the information in this book. References are provided for informational purposes only and do not constitute endorsement of any websites or other sources. Readers should be aware that the websites listed in this book may change. Always seek the advice of your physician, psychiatrist, psychologist, or other qualified health care providers with any questions you may have regarding a psychological condition or treatment, and never disregard professional mental health care advice or delay in seeking it because of something you have learned in this book. If you are considering hurting yourself or hurting someone else, you can call 911 or find the nearest hospital for support. There are many crisis hotlines to call if you need immediate help. If you are in need, contact the National Suicide Prevention Lifeline at 800.273.TALK (8255) or contact the Crisis Text Line by texting HOME to 741741.

This book is dedicated to all the courageous clients who have shared their stories with me. It was an honor to hold space with you and share your pain.

I have the deepest respect for your work.

This book is also dedicated to the majestic dream teacher, Robert Moss, and the "Journey of the Mountain Lion" that inspired the writing of this book.

Contents

Preface xi

Introduction. xv

Chapter One: You Need the ***Right*** Therapist 1
    Changes and Expectations 2
        Section 1: Change *2*
        Section 2: Why? Who? What? *3*

Chapter Two: What is therapy? 7
    Relationship and Self-Awareness 8
    Unhelpful Stories and Core Beliefs 10
    What Is Therapy For? 11
    What Are the Benefits? 12
    You Are in Charge of the Goals 14

Chapter Three: Definitions 17
    Abuse 18
    Counselor/Mental Health Therapist 18
    Court-Ordered Treatment 19
    Limits of Confidentiality 19
    Mental Health Treatment 20

Play, Art, Music, Dance, Drama and Sand Tray Therapist . 21
　　　Psychiatrist 21
　　　Psychologist 22
　　　Psychology 24
　　　Psychotropics 24

CHAPTER FOUR: Licensed Therapists 27
　　　Who Are the Therapists?. 28
　　　What Do These Letters Mean? 29
　　　Licensure 30

CHAPTER FIVE: Realities About Therapy. 33
　　　When to Seek Mental Health Treatment 34
　　　The Stigma of Mental Health 35
　　　Oversimplification in Mental Health 36
　　　Insurance Limitations on Mental Health 39

CHAPTER SIX: Commonly Asked Questions. 41
　　　How Much Does Therapy Cost?. 42
　　　How Can I Find a Therapist? 44
　　　If I Am on Medication, Do I Need Therapy? 45
　　　Is This Confidential?. 46
　　　What Happens in a Therapy Session?. 47
　　　What Is a Diagnosis? 50

CHAPTER SEVEN: Common Types of Treatment 53
　　　Behaviorism 55
　　　CBT or Cognitive Behavioral Therapy 55

Existentialism......................................56
Family Therapy 56
Gestalt and Mindfulness-Based Practice.............57
Person-Centered Work.........................58
Psychoanalytic or Psychodynamic Theory............58
Reality Theory 59
Populations 59

Chapter Eight: Couples Work......................61
   Couples Work Requires an Expert.................62
   Partner Violence..............................63

Chapter Nine: Crisis and Trauma....................65
   Crisis..66
   Trauma......................................68
   Memory and Trauma 71
   Behavior and Trauma 72
   What is EMDR?...............................75
      What Happens During the First EMDR Session?.....76
      How Many Sessions Will EMDR Take?............76

Chapter Ten: Children............................79
   The Process...................................81
   Diagnosing Your Child..........................83
   Attention Deficit Hyperactivity Disorder 83
   Conduct Disorder 84
   Reactive Attachment Disorder 84

    Treatment with PCIT................................84
    Children and Sexual Trauma 85
    Parenting 86

CHAPTER ELEVEN: Grief and Loss......................89

CONCLUSION: Being a Good Consumer 95

Referenced Websites................................99

About the Author.................................103

Preface

I wrote this book, quite simply, because I needed this guidance when I was nineteen years old. Confused and overwhelmed, I was asking, Do I Need a Therapist? This book began twenty-five years ago ...

That day in 1994 was like every other January afternoon. There was nothing remarkable or spectacular about the day. The sun was bright as it moved halfway across the sky. I ran out of the house dressed in jeans and pink Justin boots. I threw a handful of crackers in my mouth and thought, "I will grab a ginger-ale on my way to class."

There was no way to know that the next few minutes would change my life forever.

My backpack on, I ran across the street after two lanes of traffic stopped to let me cross. In my last few steps, I saw a headlight and heard a loud bang. My right leg took the impact, and I flew into traffic on the other side of the street. That car had been traveling at 35 mph; the driver never slowed down.

That street was the same street I had crossed many times. Such an unremarkable day. That single second reset the stage. My world shifted forever. Luckily, I was still alive to tell the story.

About a year earlier, before the car hit me, my father had died of pancreatic cancer. After a three-month war with his body, he passed away on my first day of school, August 1992. I was twenty years old. His death was actually a relief for me, as I knew my dad was no longer suffering from the horrors of cancer. However, when my dad died, my family exploded—everyone struggled to make sense of the loss of a powerful, amazing man.

A little over a year after my dad's death, on that cold evening in January, I got another reality check. When I was hit by that car in the crosswalk, death became very real to me. Again.

Ninety-eight percent of all pedestrian-car accidents end in fatality. I am one of the two percent alive to tell the story. That felt daunting. Many of my friends and faculty members urged me to go see a therapist. I was a college student and completely broke, so I booked a session at the campus health center. As I sat in the waiting room, I was so scared and not quite sure what would happen or what I would say. As I sat in the waiting room, I kept wanting to get up and run out the door. I could hear my heartbeat pulsing in my ears.

My first therapy session went badly.

In fact, it was awful.

The therapist was unsympathetic and formal with me. She never made eye contact while she wrote the notes in her book.

She told me that I was angry (in an accusatory voice) and asked me to "shoot" rubber bands at the window toward students as they walked by. This activity did not make any sense then, and it makes no sense now. (With twenty years of therapeutic work behind me, I can clearly state that this rubber band request serves no therapeutic purpose.)

It was a weird, confusing session.

At the time, I didn't know anything about therapy, but I knew that this experience wasn't right. I didn't want to shoot rubber bands at anyone. I wasn't mad at the students walking by, I was mad at cancer. I was mad at the driver who hit me.

I left the therapy session feeling more alone and confused than before I went. Needless to say, I did not return to the campus health center or any other mental health setting for many years. I was so put off by the experience that I needed to go to graduate school to help me understand psychology again.

I tell this story to illustrate that not all therapists are the same. Therapy can be frustrating and even unhealthy, if you find the wrong counselor. Unfortunately, clients have shared many strange requests from therapists over the years: *put all your pictures in the garage, send your daughter to boarding school, take supplements, you need to join a gym to get sober, rip up your pillows, punch a wall, quit your job, share your trauma with your children*, or *put someone's stuff on the lawn*. All these recommendations may be born of good intentions, but they may not serve the client's best interest.

In general, therapists should not tell people what to do. A good therapist should help the client to sort out what they want to do. Therapy, at its best, should empower the client to make their own decisions. In addition, the success of therapy rests with the relationship between the therapist and the client. Back in 1994, I did not feel connected to my provider or trust her guidance. This is a clear indication that the therapy would not be successful.

If you are reading this and have had a bad experience with mental health, I support your willingness to give therapy another chance. I hope this book will give you some tools and knowledge to help navigate the system a bit better.

Introduction

Jenny, I do not know how to thank you. I feel SO different! I feel like something has been removed from my brain! I feel great! My anxiety level is really down a lot! Thank you so much! I am doing good. I have learned what really happened to me when I was eight years old and feel so much better that it was not my fault and I did fight. Knowing this, I am able to deal with what is in my life right now. The thought of going to therapy was scary. You were not afraid to hear the details of my worst day. You brought me energy, joy, and humor. I never thought I could laugh while doing trauma work. You were an awesome help to me. I have a lot of love and appreciation for our time together. You will forever be in my heart for helping me move on in my life. I have more space to deal with things. Thanks again, take care. (Letter from a former client)

If you are reading this book you probably have questions about mental health services. I wrote this guide to explain what mental health is and what it isn't. By merely asking the question, "Do I need a therapist?" you are demonstrating that you are ready to go deeper into your exploration. This book is written for the nonprofessional to solve the information gap that exists about mental health. As you read this book, you will move from confused and overwhelmed to informed and clear. This guide will provide your next steps in navigating the system. By the end of your research, you will be able to sort out the benefits of receiving therapy and navigating the mental health system in the United States.

We can open this dialogue with a few simple questions.

What is the problem you hope to solve? Are you struggling with relationships? Do you dislike your body? Are you experiencing hardship within your family? Hate your job? Want to work on self-esteem or self-worth, find your strengths and abilities? You may have some fears or want to resolve upsetting feelings like restlessness, anxiety, anger, frustration, or sadness. Are you feeling overwhelmed? List a few items that you would like to change.

How do you visualize yourself after you have solved your problem? Most of my clients report that after therapy they feel peaceful, open, alive, and lighter. They may have a new awareness, improved health, or a different relationship with people or money. Write down what you will feel like after the change.

Just by answering these two questions, you have set yourself apart by determining what you want out of therapy. Armed with knowledge, I hope you will be able to make a strong choice for yourself. This book will provide clarity, so you won't be at the whims of your health insurance provider and be limited by the therapists in your insurance network. There is a very wide range in how therapists are trained, qualified, and licensed, what healing modalities they offer, and what they charge. The best indicator for successful therapy is your relationship with your therapist. In the end, you will be the best judge about what type of treatment you are seeking and which therapist can help you get there.

Introduction

Over the last nineteen years, I have been asked many questions about therapy. Many people want to know if they need to invest in counseling. You are not alone in this quest. Just Google it. In fact, the question is so common that Google's auto-complete feature will step in before you have a chance to finish typing your question. Type this into the search bar: "Do I need a the" or "Do I need the," Google will take over with "Do I need a therapist?" or "Do I need therapy?" As of today, 203 million people are looking for the answer to this question. I hope this book will be a quick guide to help you find some answers.

This book will discuss what therapy is: the goals and benefits, who the providers are, what it costs, what types of treatment will work best for you, what happens in a session, cautions, and common definitions and diagnoses. There are separate chapters dedicated to children, couples, grief, and trauma. In the back of the book, I have included an alphabetized list of websites for your reference. These include online articles and websites that were discussed in the book. Feel free to read the entire book to get a broad overview of the field of mental health, or you can just use the table of contents to find the section that interests you.

Each chapter begins with a quote from a potential or former client. I wanted you to read the client's exact words as they requested help. Their identities have been changed to protect their confidentiality. As you are reading their concerns, you may notice that it is normal to feel emotional and confused.

The mental health field is too broad to cover everything in a concise overview like this one. Here are the limitations to this book. I have left out the history of psychology, the field of psychiatry, the work of psychologists, psychiatric medication, inpatient psychiatric units, and substance-abuse treatment. I only touch briefly on couples work. The hope is that you will have enough of the basics after reading this book to do further research on your exact interests. There are many self-help books that focus on specific topics, such as addiction. However, this book is a unique approach that provides a behind-the-scenes look at the mental health system. Certain topics were chosen over others to provide you with insider information and the broadest overview. I highlighted the most common client concerns and questions. This book is specifically targeted to address the talk therapy relationship. I hope to pull back the curtain and allow you to see what happens in a mental health session.

One other note: This book looks at therapy through a western lens, specifically at the field of mental health in the United States. Mental health in other countries may look quite different.

Thank you for taking the time to read this book and learn more about therapy. This book can be your guide to help you determine how to be a good consumer of mental health services. The information in the following pages will help you understand who you want to work with and what therapy can do. I applaud you for doing a bit of research with this book. Blessings to you on this journey. You deserve to feel better and, with a little knowledge, you can gain great rewards.

CHAPTER ONE

You Need the *Right* Therapist

My ex-husband has been a "recovering" alcoholic for eight years, in and out of rehab. Will he ever get sober? He affects my children every weekend with his arrests, nervous breakdowns, and fights. I am so tired of it. Who can help me understand addiction? I am really suffering here. I don't know how much more my children can handle. Do I need to see a specialist? I need to give my children hope. They are scared he will end up dead. (Letter from a former client)

Let us start out by answering the question from the title of this book, "Do I need a therapist?" The short answer is: "Yes. We all could benefit from a therapist, a highly qualified therapist, who specializes in our specific needs." On our best days, we don't need assistance, but good therapists can offer acceptance, support, and a sense of community. Furthermore, the right therapist can help us discover our meaning and purpose in life.

If you are considering hiring a therapist, it is a good idea to find a kind, non-judgmental person who can listen to your situation. If you are living a life with pain or suffering, a good therapist can offer a safe space to sort out your concerns. However, all therapists are not created equal. So, before you book a session, let's do a deeper dive into what the field has to offer and what you may be looking for.

The questions I ask everyone seeking therapy are, "Why are you seeking a therapist and what are your expectations about treatment?" There are many therapists out there and each has their own specialty.

The most common question I am asked is, "Can you recommend someone?"

Before I answer this, I ask, "What do you hope will happen as a result of therapy? Is this short-term or long-term? Do you want someone to approve of what is happening, give you permission to continue behaving as you have been, administer medication, provide tips, or do you just want a safe space to vent?"

Changes and Expectations

Please complete this quick two-part assessment before you read on. Think about your current stressor and reflect upon how your life has changed over the last three months.

Section 1: Change

Note how many of these are true.

- My sleep is affected (I am sleeping more or less than I used to).
- My eating has changed (I am eating more or less than I used to).
- My romantic life has been affected (I fight with my partner or I am more needy than I used to be).

- My sex life has changed (I have more sex or less sex than I used to).
- My friendships have changed (I am isolating and avoiding people, or I am going out more).
- My experience at work has changed (I have become a workaholic, or I have started to hate my job and skip work).
- Are you getting sick more frequently?
- Are you falling more or having more car accidents?
- My spending habits have changed (I spend more or less than I used to).
- My spirituality has changed (I am seeking more or seeking less spiritual connection).
- My relationship with exercise has changed (I work out more or less than I used to).

Good job reflecting! If you are experiencing changes in three or more of the above areas, it may benefit you to seek out a therapist.

Section 2: Why? Who? What?

This book is about you and what you are seeking. The first question you must ask is why.

- Why am I seeking therapy?
- Do I want to change, fix, or alter something?
- Do I want someone else to change? (We are unable change others, therapy is for yourself.)
- What is my budget? How much am I willing to invest to feel better?

- Am I going to use my insurance or be willing to pay to increase the choice of therapists?
- What do I want in a therapist (male, female, short-term, body focused, or no focus on the past)?

These are the most crucial questions. Once you answer these, you are already more prepared than the majority of clients seeking therapy. Keep these answers handy as we go through the rest of the book. They will help inform you about what you are seeking.

Now we can move on to the next questions: "What is your budget? Do you have insurance?" The list of providers will reduce significantly if you have and are using insurance.

The last questions are: "Who is the therapy for? Who will be attending the sessions: the family, you and your partner or spouse, or the kids?" You want to find a therapist who specializes in your type of individual or group need. For example, not many therapists can or should do couples counseling. Couples work in the wrong hands can make the relationship issues worse. You want to find someone who specializes in the type of counseling you are seeking.

As you set out to find the right therapist, it is beneficial to find a counselor who speaks your preferred language. Using a family member or an outsider to serve as an interpreter is not recommended. An interpreter is often a barrier, as you might find it challenging to be authentic with another person in the room. Your native language is the best language to express all the emotions and the nuances of your situation. In my practice, I have found that people who are bilingual, appreciate the ability to verbalize the problem in their native language first. Even if the therapist can't understand you, it is useful to speak your concerns once in your original language, and then you can speak to the therapist in English. This process will help you feel more connected to the concern.

Before proceeding, I want to share my background, which shapes my thoughts and feelings about therapy. I am a mental health practitioner. I am a Nationally Certified, Licensed Professional Counselor in the state of Arizona. I have a PhD in Philosophy. My specialty is trauma and the long-term effects of trauma. I use Eye Movement Desensitization and Reprocessing (EMDR) as my therapeutic modality. I have been a practicing clinician since 2000, working as a mental health therapist in psychiatric units, treatment centers, spas, employee assistance programs, licensed behavioral health facilities, universities, and private practice. In addition, I have served as the Clinical Director and College Chair for a renowned university that has CACREP, a national accreditation for the training of master's students. I taught courses for counselors and ran a clinic for master's level interns to practice their skills.

While my experiences have opened my eyes to the great work that counselors can do, I am also aware that not all counselors have the same abilities or skill sets. Many clients I have spoken with over the years have had negative experiences with counseling.

The questions in this chapter are just the first, basic questions you will want to answer before you seek a therapist. You will also need to understand a little about what therapy is and what it is not, in order to feel empowered to pick the right provider and ask them the right questions. That is what we will look at in the next chapter.

CHAPTER TWO

WHAT IS THERAPY?

So, I was very angry last night. I am not sure if it was apparent to my husband. But I was very frustrated. I spent all day thinking about it and trying to figure out why I had a huge reaction to him. I am not really mad at him, but I was angry. I have reached a tipping point where I am done being dismissed and abused. I have felt VERY alone during these last 5 months. I feel that his response to my frustration/anger has been dismissive at times, it comes across as flip. He hasn't heard my pain, my anguish, my suffering. This has been a terrible year. My anger is here, it says, WHY do I always have to be the one that walks away from an abuser???? Why are people allowed to terrorize me and everyone tells me to walk away? Why can't someone agree with me? I do want to stop fighting, I am tired. But honestly, I just want someone to see me, hear me, and accept my full range of emotions. I do not have this in my life. I want someone to say, "I see you fighting the good fight and I am sorry it is constant. You must be exhausted." Like I said, I am not mad at him. But I am mad. I am exhausted. Why did I grow up with parents that fight? I don't want to fight. I feel like I am in Ground Hog Day. I am so tired. (Letter from a former client)

Relationship and Self-Awareness

Therapy is profound. It is the act of being heard, truly heard, by another person without judgement. When you find the right therapist, you will be able to express yourself freely and find the answers you are seeking within yourself. Self-awareness is a critical piece of counseling, but we also need a solid relationship with our therapist to help us go deeper.

We all have the ability to become self-aware of our habits and fears. We have the potential to lower our walls and see the truth, but we may need someone to create a safe space for us to reflect and explore. When we feel controlled, we control our situation and others. When we are scared, our brains are flooded with emotions and we may not make good decisions. It is beneficial to find a good therapist who can help us break down these barriers, and serve as an anchor, a neutral, safe person who will be there to reassure us when the work is hard.

Of course, every therapist is human and imperfect. They have no magical powers, but they are trained to listen and engage you in critical thinking. Therapy is like having a conversation with an impartial person who can "hear your emotions." A good therapist will not tell you what to do. She will reflect back to you your ideas and values. Once you do the self-exploration, you need to trust the person you are sharing with.

That being said, the most important feature is the *relationship* and the trust you feel with your therapist. If you trust the person you are working with, you can explore concerns at a deeper level. You need a counselor who is not afraid to hear the details of your worst day. If you feel judged or your therapist changes the subject when you are speaking, this is an indicator for you. Therapy should be a safe space to explore ideas. You should feel seen and heard. If you feel judged or pushed aside, find another provider. There are so many therapists—take the time to find one who fits you perfectly.

One goal of therapy is to become aware of ourselves. But how can we do this if we feel nervous about what may happen? In self-awareness work, you are leaving your comfort zone and walking into the unknown. Your emotions are a signal that this is important, challenging work; you may, indeed, dig up pain and you may feel upset. Your therapist can help you see, hear yourself, raise awareness, find the tools … but ultimately, you will take responsibility for your own growth. This is another reason why it is so important to have a good relationship with your counselor; it will benefit you to share your fears and your pain with someone who will support you.

While counseling can lead to increased self-awareness, new tools, and a calmer outlook, there are no guarantees of what you will experience. You may uncover things that you were avoiding. Counseling may involve discussing upsetting events, and you may experience uncomfortable feelings. In fact, therapy is most useful when you are distressed. For example, if your depression is affecting your job or your relationship, therapy is a great place to sort that out.

After a few sessions, therapy should not make you feel worse. Sorting through your concerns usually provides some element of clarity. If you feel terrible after each session, this may be an indicator to help you determine whether or not you have found the right therapist. Ultimately, therapy is the experience of being heard and seen so that you can engage in self-awareness work.

Unhelpful Stories and Core Beliefs

One of the main features of counseling is to explore the unhelpful stories we tell ourselves. These stories were originally created to help us avoid pain. For example, you may tell yourself the story, "I am fat." This story then "protects" you from getting hurt in dating. If you believe that you are fat, you might not date. Another story you could tell yourself is "all men cheat." If you tell yourself this, you are again trying to protect yourself from getting hurt. This is normal, we all want to avoid pain. However, when we try to avoid pain, we create weird coping strategies. Weird coping strategies could include:

- avoiding people
- chaotic relationships
- drinking
- destructive patterns
- being mean to ourselves
- over-shopping, over-eating, or over-sexing
- shutting down
- working too much
- worrying excessively

When we engage in these strategies, the mind will create a story to try and make sense of our behaviors. Remember it does this to "help" us stay safe. For example, you may say to yourself, "I am dating my ex again because I can't be alone." Unfortunately, these stories we create may become obstacles to our success in life. For example, the previous statement, "I can't be alone," is a belief that may be counterproductive. A thought like this one can easily become fixed as we repeat it to ourselves. It can transform into what is called a core belief. In effect, the stories we tell ourselves, based in pain and fear, can confuse us. We can confuse what feels dangerous and what *is* actually dangerous! As such, it is so beneficial to have a conversation with someone who is trained to see these coping strategies.

Therapy requires working on ourselves. Unfortunately, you cannot change someone else. (Save yourself time and energy if you want therapy to change someone else.) Therapy requires you to look at your thoughts, emotions, and actions all with honesty and patience. It is not a passive process. Therapy is like learning a new skill. It will require you to put in the time and practice.

At first, therapy might feel vulnerable, weird, or uncomfortable. When you begin to discuss the stories that you tell yourself or the events that you have been avoiding, this can be difficult. Often, these are the first areas a therapist will want to explore with you. She will ask you to reflect on yourself.

I can assure you, the hard work is worth it. Therapy can be an enormous gift. You can release anger, sadness, and anxiety. You can change bad habits, have more mental clarity, and feel better! If you are willing to be honest and explore, you can benefit greatly.

What Is Therapy For?

What will you discuss in session? In therapy, you may talk about old childhood pain or you might explore stresses in your life now. The topics that you might explore may seem endless:

- abuse, addictions, adoption, anxiety,
- behavioral problems, birth, body image, bullying,
- change of life, coping strategies, communication,

- death, depression, domestic violence, dreams,
- early childhood,
- failing, family, fears, feelings, finding your purpose, friendships,
- gender, grief,
- infidelity,
- loss,
- manipulation, marriage, money, moving,
- pain, parenting, phobias, power dynamics,
- racial inequity, rape, relationships, religion,
- school, sex, sexuality, social injustice, stress, substance use,
- trauma,
- upsetting patterns,
- weight, work

The list goes on and on. You can discuss anything! Therapy should be a neutral, safe place to discuss things that maybe you wouldn't share with a spouse, friend, or neighbor. A good way to use your time in session is to explore fears and concerns that you wouldn't tell other people in your life. Therapy is a confidential, safe space.

What Are the Benefits?

There are many benefits from participating in therapy. Therapists can provide support and teach a variety of problem-solving skills and coping strategies. Therapists can encourage personal growth, explore relationships, discuss family concerns, or look at marriage issues. A counselor can simply be a non-judgmental person who will listen to the hassles of your daily life. Therapists can provide new perspectives on difficult problems. Often, they can point you in the direction of a solution.

Over the years, I have heard the following kinds of statements from clients after they have participated in therapy:

- "I understand myself better."
- "I have figured out my goals, values, and purpose."
- "I have learned how to have better relationships with others."
- "I have improved my communication, my listening skills."
- "I feel more at peace."
- "I took a look at my dysfunctional behaviors and I learned some new positive behaviors."
- "I fixed my problems in my family, in my marriage."
- "I am more patient, less reactive at work."
- "I have figured out how to stop my road rage."
- "I feel better about myself; I guess I had low self-esteem."
- "I took a hard look at my family and realized why I do what I do."
- "I found out that I am stronger than I believed. I am a survivor, not a victim."
- "I have been afraid to get married for so long. Now I have clarity about why."
- "I understand why I began drinking; it all makes sense now."
- "I have had anxiety my entire life. Therapy helped me learn new skills to manage my stress."

- "I was raised in a military family. I had no idea what emotions were. I used to be afraid when people would cry. I now understand myself and my emotions."
- "I needed help after my mom died, I was a wreck. Therapy helped me remember myself."
- "I don't avoid people anymore."
- "I am a better mom now."
- "I make my own decisions. I can leave situations that are unhealthy."

As you can see from this list of testimonials, therapy can have a positive impact on so many aspects of your life. The truth is, therapy can be life-changing. A good counselor can provide insight and help you remember your internal strength.

You Are in Charge of the Goals

The ultimate goal of therapy is for you to understand yourself better. It is so beneficial for you to understand what you like, what annoys you, and why certain people create strong emotional responses in you. The goal is that, when the storms of life happen, you have an understanding of why you are reacting the way you are, you have some tools to help you figure things out, and you have some kindness for yourself as you face your challenges. Hopefully, therapy can help you become stronger and better able to process and reflect upon what is happening in your life during times of trouble.

Therapy should not create a co-dependent relationship between you and your therapist. You are not entering into a contract for the rest of your life. You can stop going any time. Most people stop counseling when they remember their own strength and begin to chart their own course.

Each person has different concerns and goals for therapy, so therapy will be different for each person, depending on what they are seeking. You and your therapist will likely set goals during the first or second session. You can decide if you want to take part in short-term work or look at earlier family patterns, which may take longer. In general, most sessions will focus on the current concerns happening in your life, but it is possible that your therapist may examine your history as it pertains to the current issue affecting your life. Each week you may report to your therapist how the sessions have affected you, such as what improvements or frustrations have risen as a result of the previous therapy session.

Short-term therapy works best if you just want to look at one specific issue. Long-term therapy works best if you are exploring complex issues and those that span your lifetime. Most people see a counselor once a week for fifty minutes a session. Some counselors give homework. Others ask you to keep a journal, to record thoughts or dreams. You will get better results in therapy if you are honest with yourself and actively participate in the process.

One of the most important outcomes of therapy is for you to take the insights you discover during your sessions and apply them to your daily life. This can take many forms. You may write letters, have family meetings, keep a journal, record personal thoughts, explore your reactions to things, or try new activities. Your therapist will want you to take personal responsibility for choices you have made and make positive improvement. In addition, a good therapist will be patient and explore the blocks that stop you from moving forward.

Therapy is not a quick fix. A therapist will listen with an open mind and reflect back what they have heard. The counselor may offer insight or perspective. They may just listen with empathy and kindness. You will go as deep or as real as you want to go.

As I stated at the beginning of this chapter, therapy is the profound act of being heard by another person without judgment. It may take a month or two to establish trust and allow you to feel safe with your therapist. There is no magic right or wrong answer. You will share your frustrations and hopefully gain insight about your life and your concerns.

This type of therapy is called person-centered treatment or client-centered treatment. (As a side note: other types of treatment can focus on specific areas of concern and the therapist's style is more directive.) We will learn about other types of treatment in chapter seven, "Common Types of Treatment." Ultimately, you will determine how successful therapy is based on how much you participate in the process and put into practice what you learn.

CHAPTER THREE

DEFINITIONS

I gave the vault keys to a bank customer today on accident! I drove my car into a closed garage door! I feel like I am losing my mind. Half of the time I don't even know what I am saying. They put me on probation at work. I am afraid I am going to lose my job. I feel nuts. What if my husband leaves me? I can sense that his patience is running out. I walk around my kitchen from four to six in the morning trying to remember what I am supposed to be doing. Did I come in here for laundry? Coffee? What am I doing? It is a miracle I am showered and dressed when I come to work every day. You have to help me. I can't keep track of anything. I am crying all day. I can't stop. I have had to leave meetings. (Letter from a former client)

We often use words like "therapy" with an assumption of a common definition. This chapter will explain how I am defining these often-used terms. It is helpful to understand some basic terms when you are seeking a therapist. These definitions are in alphabetical order for ease of reading.

Abuse

Abuse occurs when one person uses their power and control to harm another person. Abuse can be verbal, physical, sexual, emotional, or financial in nature. It can be subtle, or it can be obvious. It can happen one time or it can extend for years. Abuse is illegal in the United States. Yet it is a huge problem. The National Coalition Against Domestic Violence cites that "1 in 4 women and 1 in 9 men experience severe intimate partner physical violence, intimate partner sexual violence, and/or intimate partner stalking."

If you think you are experiencing abuse, there are many sources that provide support.

- National Sexual Assault Hotline at RAINN: 1-800-656-HOPE (4673)
- National Domestic Violence line at 1-800-799-7233
- Elder Abuse
- National Child Abuse hotline: 1800-4ACHILD or 1800-422-4453
- Trans Lifeline: (877) 565-8860
- Bullying at Upstand
- To write love on her arms
- Children's Bureau at An Office of the Administration for Children & Families

Counselor/Mental Health Therapist

You will find that these terms are used interchangeably: *counselor*, *therapist*, *clinician*, *psychotherapist*, *service provider*, and *practitioner*. All of these terms refer to a licensed person who provides direct service to clients in clinics, private practice, community health centers, and schools. When referenced in this book, this person is a trained, master's level or higher, mental health practitioner who holds a license in their state. They charge between $125 and $250 an hour. For more information, see chapter four, under the heading, "What Do Those Letters Mean?"

Court-Ordered Treatment

The legal system may require you to see a court-mandated therapist for a variety of reasons. For example, you may need documentation from a therapist during a custody dispute or you received a citation for driving under the influence (DUI). If you are directed by a judge to seek treatment, this is called court-ordered or court-mandated treatment.

Before you attend your first counseling session, make sure you ask the provider whether or not they will write the documents you need for court. Many therapists do not offer this specialty service, so ask when you call to book your session. The counselors who do submit documents to the court usually have specialty training or expertise. This service will often involve an extra fee for having the therapist testify in court or for writing the required paperwork.

Some legal disputes are not resolved in the courtroom and, instead, are resolved through an arbitration process call mediation. Mediation is conducted by specialized, trained professionals who have certification or experience in this field. Not all therapists can do this specialized work, and not all mediators are therapists. Often this service is contracted through your employer or the courts may mandate it. The court will often give you a list of approved providers.

Limits of Confidentiality

Confidentiality means your therapist will keep private the information you share with her. As a client, you have the right to withhold or release information about yourself to other individuals or agencies. However, a therapist must have a signed release form from you before he or she can release any information about you.

In some situations, there are limits to your confidentiality. Your therapist will not be bound by confidentiality in the following situations:

- A court subpoenas information from your counselor.
- Your counselor is mandated by the state to report abuse, neglect, exploitation of minors, exploitation of the elderly, exploitation of disabled persons, sexual exploitation; and any individuals who are a danger to themselves or others.
- State laws have specific confidentiality provisions. For example, Arizona has a law that allows legal guardians to bypass confidentiality for people under the age of eighteen. Therefore, a guardian could request a therapist's chart about a minor child.

If confidentiality is important to you, you will want to check with state laws and regulations about the limits of confidentiality before you begin sessions with your therapist.

Mental Health Treatment

These terms will often be used interchangeably: *treatment, talk therapy, therapy, psychotherapy, psychological therapies, interventions, mental health services, therapeutic procedures,* and *treatment plan*. Although these terms mean different things, they are used to indicate treatment of a client.

Play, Art, Music, Dance, Drama and Sand Tray Therapist

The terms *play*, *art*, *music*, *dance*, *drama*, and *sand tray* before a therapist's title indicates a master's level clinician with specialty training in these areas. Therapists often undergo additional training, schooling, exams, apprenticeships, and practice after they complete their master's degree in order to become proficient in these specialties. These specialties are called *therapeutic modalities*, and they are often used to treat children, although many adults can benefit from these creativity-based treatment models. When considering a therapist who has one of these specialties, it is important to make sure she has a license to practice in your state. You can learn more about these modalities by visiting the following websites:

- Association for Play Therapy
- American Art Therapy Association
- American Music Therapy Association
- American Dance Therapy Association
- North American Drama Therapy Association
- Sandplay Therapists of America

More information about these specialties can be found in chapter ten, "Children."

Psychiatrist

A psychiatrist is a medical doctor. A psychiatrist attended medical school, completed medical internship or residency, took their state's examination to become a medical doctor, and is licensed in the state where they practice. One of the major distinctions between a therapist and a psychiatrist is that a psychiatrist can prescribe medications. Some psychiatrists are trained as counselors in addition to their medical license. However, most psychiatrists do not provide talk therapy. If they do offer you a fifty-minute talk therapy session, ask if they have specific training in counseling or behavioral techniques.

Treatment with a psychiatrist generally begins with one or two intake sessions, during which the psychiatrist will ask you many questions and then prescribe medication based on their assessment. They also monitor patients taking medications. This monitoring is done in fifteen-minute appointments, once every three months. They check to see if patients are experiencing side effects to the prescribed medication. Psychiatrists charge approximately $180 to $300 per session.

If you want to see a psychiatrist, you may want to check with your insurance provider to find one within your network. You can find out more about psychiatry on the American Psychiatric Association website.

Psychologist

A psychologist has a specialty in psychological assessment and testing. They may or may not have earned their master's in counseling. They have their doctorate in psychology, they completed an internship, they took a state examination, and are licensed in the states in which they practice. They have been taught to administer, score, and document psychological assessments. One familiar type of psychological assessment is an IQ test, but there are many different types. Their field of study may have focused on testing specific groups of people, and they may not have taken courses in counseling or talk therapy. During a session, a psychologist will ask good questions, administer tests, and interpret the test results. They charge between $150 and $300 an hour, depending on the length of the assessment and analysis time.

Some psychologists work for the courts or agencies that require formal evaluations. For example, in most states, before you can get gastric bypass surgery, you will need to see a psychologist for an evaluation. After the evaluation, they will write an assessment and send this to your doctor. In addition, some schools or employers may require you to have a psychological assessment of some kind.

If you want to see a psychologist, you should check with your insurance provider to see which providers are in your network and what assessments the insurance provider will cover. Procedures for administering assessments vary, but you can assume your visit to a psychologist will include an intake appointment followed by three to six sessions, during which the psychologist will ask you many questions. These assessments take hours to complete and write.

Psychologists became popular during the First World War, because they were employed by the United States Army to administer standardized intelligence and aptitude tests. Over two million soldiers received these assessments, which were used to place soldiers in their jobs. The military still administers these tests today to all armed forces and civilian settings.

Some psychologists assess weaknesses and disorders in children and administer tests in school settings. These providers will probably not offer talk therapy. If they do, you will want to ask if they have training in counseling or behavioral techniques. For more information about psychologists, visit the website of the American Psychological Association (APA).

Psychology

Generally speaking, psychology is the study of human behavior, but it is a complex discipline that is over a hundred years old and has broad definitions. Often, the words *behavior* and *science* are mentioned in the definition. William James in 1890 called psychology the study of *mental* life. John B. Watson in 1913 stated that psychology is the "prediction and control" of human *behavior*. We should always include the intention of the founding professional organization into its definition. The primary focus of the APA is to advance psychology as a science. Psychology can also be defined by what psychologists do. Therefore, it can be defined as the study of human behavior and how people relate to their environment.

In this book, I explore psychology as a practice that expands, enriches, and liberates people from unhealthy, static patterns of behavior. I look at psychology as a field that informs a counselor's training and practice.

Psychotropics

Psychotropics is a term given to medications that are administered to produce specific mental health outcomes and mood regulation. There are many classifications of psychotropics. Most of them affect neurotransmitters and the central nervous system. Psychotropics include the following, but there are many others in addition to those listed here:

- analgesics, anesthetics, antidementia drugs, antidepressants, antiepileptics, antipsychotics, anxiolytics,
- hypnotics,
- monoamine oxidase inhibitors (MAOIs), mood stabilizers,

- noradrenaline reuptake inhibitors, noradrenergic and selective serotonergic antidepressants,
- selective serotonin reuptake inhibitor (SSRIs), serotonin-norepinephrine reuptake inhibitors (SNRIs),
- tricyclic antidepressants (TCAs)

Many psychotropics have severe side effects, such as mood deregulation, sexual dysfunction, sleep disorders, and weight gain. If you want to learn more about these medications, you should visit a reputable psychiatrist who specializes in psychotropics. You can also learn more about a specific drug by visiting the FDA Drug page.

If you have been prescribed psychotropic medication, it is vital that you **do not stop taking your medication and do not change your dosage without the express permission of the psychiatrist who prescribed it.** Work with your doctor if you want to change your treatment path. If you make the slightest change, even the time of day you take your medication, **it could be harmful, even increasing suicidal thoughts**. A great deal of research in this area shows that these psychotropic medications work best when the client is using them in combination with talk therapy sessions. To learn more about psychotropics, see chapter five, under the section called "Oversimplification in Mental Health."

CHAPTER FOUR

Licensed Therapists

I think I need to do some deeper work. When we last met, I wasn't ready to look at the underlying issue, but I am now. What am I doing with my life? I am fifty years old and I have NOTHING to show for it! No kids, no marriage, no house, no career ... What am I doing? I made all of these decisions. I don't want a white picket fence, a kid and a dog ... but I thought I would be feeling ok at this point in my life. I live pay check to pay check. It's like I am at the top of the hill looking down. There is more behind me than in front of me. I will never retire. What do I want to do? Clearly the plan is not working. I almost quit today. I have a real apathy for what I do, I sort of just did the job because I was offered it. I am good at it, I guess, I just don't like it. I need to examine what is going on in my head. I need to find happiness. (Letter from a former client)

Who Are the Therapists?

You will find many different terms for those who provide mental health services:

- adult service providers, art therapists, associate counselors,
- behavioral health providers, behavioral health technicians,
- child life specialists, child protective services, counselors,
- equine therapists
- forensic interviewers,
- hospice social workers,
- intake specialists, interns,
- lay counselors, life management specialists
- marriage and family therapists, mental health practitioners, mental health providers,
- peer coaches, play therapists, psychiatrists, psychologists,
- shrinks, social workers, Stephen ministers,
- therapists

And that is not all of them! The list seems endless. Professionals earn different degrees and attain specific licensures in order to use these terms. They also charge different fees. In the area of talk therapy, three types of therapists are most common:

- Licensed Independent Clinical Social Worker (LICSW)
- Licensed Marriage and Family Therapist (LMFT)
- Licensed Professional Counselor (LPC)

Professionals with these titles have several things in common. They all completed three-year master's degrees and nine-month internships, passed state licensing exams, and finished two-year apprenticeships before becoming licensed in their state to practice therapy. Some states allow all three of these types of therapists to assess and provide clients with a diagnosis, such as the state of Arizona. (The terms *therapist*, *clinician*, and *counselor* are used interchangeably in this book to indicate this master level of provider.)

What Do These Letters Mean?

As a quick example, I will use my name and titles. On my counseling business card, my name is Jenny Simon, MC, LPC, NCC.

- MC is my degree. I have a Master of Counseling in Community Counseling degree. Most counselors will list their master's degree after their name.
- The "L" after someone's name means that they are licensed in the state that they provide counseling. LPC, in Arizona, refers to a Licensed Professional Counselor.
- NCC refers to a National Certified Counselor according to the National Board of Certified Counselors.

Most counselors list their master's initials behind their name first:

- MA (Master of Arts)
- MC (Master of Counseling)
- MEd (Master of Education)
- MS (Master of Science)

Then, after their master's degree, counselors list their licensure:

- LICSW (Licensed Independent Clinical Social Worker)
- LMFT (Licensed Marriage and Family Counselor)
- LPC (Licensed Professional Counselor)

Newly graduated students who are apprentices have an A, for associate, in their initials. These clinicians will be working under a licensed provider for at least two years.

- ASW (Associate Social Worker)
- LAC (Licensed Associate Counselor)
- LAMFT (Licensed Associate Marriage and Family Therapist)

Addiction providers have special letters too.

- LASAC (Licensed Associate Substance Abuse Counselor)
- LISAC (Licensed Independent Substance Abuse Counselor)

Providers who want to counsel over the phone use BC-TMH, which means Board Certified TeleMental Health Provider.

Licensure

All counselors in the United States must be licensed. In order to obtain licensure, every state requires individuals to complete a board-approved master's program (three years of college, as well as a nine-month internship), take and pass a state and/or national exam, and then apply for an associate license (which involves two years of apprenticeship under a licensed provider). After completing all of these requirements, an individual can apply for licensure. In case you are counting, that is FIVE full years, including college, internship, exams, and apprenticeship before anyone can become an independently licensed mental health provider!

All licensed counselors with either a master's degree or a doctorate have state-specific licensures, meaning that these licenses do not transfer from state to state. Like a lawyer, counselors must be licensed in the state in which they practice. If a therapist moves, they will need to apply for licensure in their new state. Make sure that your counselor has a license to practice in your state. If you choose to receive counseling from someone who is still an intern, ask them for their supervisor's state license number.

Each state has a board that reviews licenses. This board serves the public interest, so if a counselor has committed an ethics violation and is brought before this board, there will be a public record on file. The following associations provide information for each type of counselor's code of ethics and scope of practice.

- American Association for Marriage and Family Therapy
- American Counseling Association
- National Association of Social Workers
- National Board for Certified Counselors

CHAPTER FIVE

Realities About Therapy

Hey, what's up? Sorry to bother you. I need help, I have a new therapist. I guess I like her. She is weird, she ate lunch during my session. She held my hand and cried. I guess she is ok. She told me to put my pictures of Dan in the garage. I am not sure why. She seems to think that when I see the pictures, I get sad. The truth is I am sad all of the time. I do not want to die, I am not suicidal, but honestly it would be ok if I didn't make it out of this surgery. To be honest, life is hard without Dan. It is challenging to just get up. I hate paying bills, dealing with the house, and having to deal with the stupid doctor's bills. I am done. I feel so exhausted, even my teeth hurt. I wish God would have taken me with him. I can't do anything. I just have no desire to do anything. Everything feels so hard. Maybe I won't call the therapist back, she called me sweetie. I don't feel very sweet right now. What should I do? I need my sessions to be covered by insurance. I can't afford you or I would come back. (Letter from a former client)

When to Seek Mental Health Treatment

This section is dedicated to troubles and circumstances that are above and beyond minor changes in daily life. This section contains red flags and warnings that indicate that you would benefit from professional help. You should go see a therapist for the following reasons:

- if you have an eating disorder or an unrealistic body image; you throw up after eating; you severely restrict calories; you overeat; or you have had multiple plastic surgeries to improve the appearance of your body.
- if you are engaging in substance abuse; are misusing drugs (legal and illegal), or you are drinking three or more alcoholic beverages a day.
- if you experienced trauma as a child and you have attempted to forget about it and move on.
- if you see or hear things that other people don't see or hear.
- if you have traumatic flashbacks of car accidents, violence, natural disaster, or abuse.
- if your sleep is disturbed due to recurring images.
- if you have a fear or phobia that limits your daily interaction with the world.
- if your mood (anger, sadness, anxiety) is interfering with your job, your relationships, your friendships, or your ability to handle daily activities.
- if someone suggests journaling and you are too afraid to write; if you have a fear about putting things into words; or if you don't want to think about it, even less write it or speak it.

- if you have a medical condition that you believe was or is being caused by stress.
- if you are engaging in self-harm (cutting, burning, reckless behavior, or driving excessive speeds on the freeway).
- if you have addictions that help you avoid life or cost you, such as gambling, video gaming, the internet, shopping, sex, porn, drugs, or alcohol.
- if you think that you are being mistreated by a romantic partner. Fifty percent of all women have experienced relationship violence (verbal or physical or sexual).
- if you are blaming yourself for something. Blame stops you from helping yourself.
- if you are grieving the loss of someone or something that you can't talk openly about.
- if you are minimizing or not thinking about a problem.
- if you are isolating from others.
- if you have changed your behavior in a major way in the areas of eating, sleeping, socializing, work, or exercise.
- if you have thoughts about hurting or killing yourself.
- if you have thoughts about hurting or killing someone else.

If you are in need, contact the National Suicide Prevention Lifeline at 800.273.TALK (8255) or contact the Crisis Text Line by texting HOME to 741741.

The Stigma of Mental Health

Having good mental health is like having good physical health. To attain physical health, we may need to change our diet, sleep patterns, or exercise habits. We may see a doctor, if we don't feel well. It is a good, healthy choice to seek help from a medical provider.

We should hold the same standard for mental health.

Even if you have been able to solve your problems in the past, there are times when we need extra help. Seeking mental health does not mean that you are weak, crazy, broken, or damaged. Therapy is a tool for self-care. We should reach out and be heard. There is strength in recognizing that you need a second opinion. Therapy can shift your thoughts, ideas, and mental patterns forever, or it can be a short power boost to get you through a rough patch.

We need to stop using terms like *crazy* and *insane* to describe people when they suffer under the weight of life's challenges. We need to encourage our friends and loved ones to get help when they are struggling. If you are reading this book, I assume that you already know how important mental health can be. Thank you for being an ally to help reduce the stigma of mental health. The National Alliance on Mental Illness website provides a great deal of information on mental illness.

Oversimplification in Mental Health

Unfortunately, the mental health system has some concerns that the consumer should be aware of. One area of potential concern is your health insurance provider. Many health insurance plans have a "fee for service" limit on the number of sessions they will cover each year. These types of limits have pushed the mental health field toward brief, solution-focused work, but many therapists feel that this approach does not give them enough time to get to know and effectively treat their clients. A client will receive services based on their level of need. The more critical your diagnosis, the more sessions your insurance provider will cover. In effect, managed care and insurance companies are driving treatment goals. This dynamic is allowing individuals to become more and more unwell before they can get the care they need.

As such, it is important to speak with your therapist about all of the nuances and requirements of your insurance plan. In my own practice, I do not work with insurance companies, because I feel that approach gives my clients greater freedom. I don't have to assign them a specific diagnosis or adhere to one-size-fits-all treatment plans. I also know from speaking to other professionals that many clients choose to pay out of pocket to avoid this dynamic.

This dynamic grows out of our expectations today in modern life. Many clients seeking therapy have watched crime shows and have come to expect a certain amount of technology to help solve their mental health concerns. We are convinced that the newest developments in brain research will help us erase bad memories or shape our wild child into an angelic cherub. We are addicted to the idea of a quick fix. We love the idea of "happy" medication, and many clients call their psychotropics "happy pills."

This hope for a quick fix is reflected through the concept of evidenced-based treatment. Evidenced-based treatments are behaviorally based therapies that aim to change behavior quickly. Insurance companies will only fund evidence-based treatment. On the surface, this sounds wonderful. Why wouldn't you want fast, evidenced-based treatment? The short answer is, because it is restrictive, and this type of therapy doesn't cover the range of human experience.

Current science can only evaluate what it can observe and measure. Therefore, a client's inner experience and emotions are often ignored. I have the deepest respect for the scientific community and its desire to prove why certain treatments work; however, science is currently unable to evaluate a client's emotions. So, the evidenced-based movement always defaults to behavior as its only measurement tool. Can you imagine being evaluated only by what you do, not by what you think or feel? I believe that the human experience is more complex than a set of behaviors.

You may also ask, "How does having a fifty-minute therapy session about client feelings and emotions fit into this model?" It doesn't. The unfortunate reality is that having an in-depth conversation with a neutral party, using talk therapy, may not be recognized by insurance companies as evidenced-based treatment. As a result, mental health providers may have to give you a diagnosis and provide an evidence-based treatment plan to encourage your insurance company to pay for services.

The truth of the matter is we really have a great deal to learn about the human brain, human emotions, and how we store and retrieve memory. And drugs are far from a simple, quick fix. Although millions of people use psychotropic drugs, the negative side effects are enormous and dangerous. Psychotropics wash the brain, central nervous system, and body in chemicals. Common side effects include weight gain, sexual dysfunction, sleep disorders, hormone changes, and dramatic mood swings. When I worked in a psychiatric inpatient ward, I saw patients try as many as twelve medications to get the right formula. Psychotropics are far from an exact science. I once heard a psychiatrist say, "Using psychotropics is like opening a car's hood and pouring oil on top of the entire engine. We don't yet know where exactly to pour the oil so it will do the most good."

Of course, some psychotropics are very beneficial and needed. But, consumers push for psychotropics because they want to feel good. They hope that a pill will allow them to bypass the difficult stuff: the process of looking at the underlying cause of their issues. Unfortunately, psychotropics aren't a magic wand, and some side effects are very debilitating and can even lead to death.

A word of warning, if you are taking psychotropics, please check with your doctor before changing your dosage, taking new medications, or changing the time of day you take them. The slightest alteration can cause massive changes and lead to potentially dangerous consequences. It is best to use psychotropics in combination with talk therapy.

Insurance Limitations on Mental Health

Here is a tongue-in-cheek snapshot of the oversimplified psychology system. It is intended to highlight some of the problems that underpin the field of psychology.

As we've seen, insurance companies currently regulate how many therapeutic sessions a client can have. A client may only have three to eight sessions (depending on their insurance plan) to "fix" their issues. Let's look at this dynamic through the lens of child therapy.

A family contacts a therapist to reduce their child's anxiety. The insurance company limits the therapist to three to eight sessions, so the therapist ignores the emotional and mental state of the child and focuses on behavioral symptoms. The insurance company will want proof of the child's disorder and asks the therapist to identify a behavioral outcome. So, the therapist will give the client an overly simplistic diagnosis and apply an equally simple, evidence-based treatment plan. The therapist will use an evidence-based checklist of behaviors, techniques that reinforce or punish certain behaviors, and look for symptom reduction, all without exploring the child's underlying emotions.

Basically, if the family wants the insurer to cover the treatment, the therapist's hands are tied.

But an evidence-based strategy will often fail to address complex, underlying factors that are causing the child to struggle. When a therapist is forced to use a "cookie-cutter" treatment plan, it will often fail to address what's going on under the surface. The therapist might even end up referring the child to another expert who will administer medication until the client is drugged into behaving properly. If the medications fail, the therapist can then blame the expert.

The medical insurance system is broken in the United States and, partially as a result, the mental health system has suffered the same fate. As consumers, we can avoid the pitfalls of this damaged system by asking questions, by arming ourselves with knowledge and information, and by paying for our own services to avoid having an insurance company dictate our treatment. We can also talk to our therapists about this damaging dynamic. We can demand great care and avoid this oversimplified way of looking at complex concerns. You deserve thorough treatment. Ask your provider for it!

CHAPTER SIX

Commonly Asked Questions

Help me! I would love to believe that my best work-friend is clean, she tells me she is. But I don't believe her. Recently her humor has become aggressive and sad. It's not funny, no lightness. She is angry with no silliness. She makes jabs at me at work and she has disappeared. I know she is using again. She is everything I don't need, a flakey person who disappears and attempts to hide or lie about what she is doing. She is unable to show up due to her own self-absorbedness. It feels like a break up. There is a loss of companionship but also a fear of betrayal. I feel uneasy. She knows everything about me. I told her to show up and not ghost out. She went from fifty-two texts a day to utter silence or mean humor. Two weeks have gone by without a text or an email to say, "Hey, I am stressed out." I guess I was used. I was useful until I wasn't. If you break up with someone, they go away. With a work friend, you see her every day. With an addict you care, and it sucks. What am I supposed to do? Why do I always trust the wrong people? (Letter from a former client)

How Much Does Therapy Cost?

Most counselors see clients once a week for fifty minutes. Sessions can cost between $65 to $250 for that therapeutic hour of fifty minutes. Interns should charge lower fees as they are new to the field and they are being supervised. Despite the conversation from the previous chapter, using medical insurance is often your best way to reduce costs. Please review the section called "Insurance Limitations on Mental Health" in chapter five.

Prior to finding a therapist, call your insurance company to get details about your mental health coverage. Find out how many sessions they will allow, any co-pay you will need to cover, and what providers are included in your plan's network. Once you have a list of potential providers, search for their names on websites like *Psychology Today*. You will often be able to see a picture of the therapist and read a little bit about their style and personality. The Psychology Today website is a great place to find a list of local therapists. Begin by entering your zip code in the search field and then narrow the results by entering practitioner specialty or by entering your health insurance provider.

Another inexpensive way to get mental health services is to check with your employer to see if they have an Employee Assistance Program (EAP). Through an EAP, you can usually get free, time-limited sessions. Normally a local counselor will contract with your company's EAP to provide between three and eight sessions for you or a family member. Your EAP counselor will also make referrals for you, if you need medication, specific assessments, court-ordered treatment, and acute substance-abuse intervention.

As a side note: just as with every other type of therapy, therapists that are contracted through your EAP must keep your information confidential. They are not permitted to disclose information about you to your employer unless you sign a consent form that allows your employer to access this information.

Many mental health providers offer group counseling sessions. Group sessions often cost much less than one-to-one therapy—$10 to $50 a session. Therapists create groups based on common themes and can help you connect with others who are struggling with similar concerns. There is a wide range of topics for which you may be able to find a group:

- anger management
- domestic violence
- grief
- men's groups
- parenting
- substance use
- women's groups

Group therapy may be a great choice for you to save some money and get support.

A quick note about Alcoholics Anonymous (AA) and other peer-support groups: these groups are free and are not regulated by your state's behavioral health system. In other words, there are no state standards applied to these programs. They are peer-run and adhere to the guidelines of the twelve-step philosophy. These groups can be helpful, but they are not a substitute for therapy. They only offer peer support. You should seek out a licensed provider for counseling, especially if you have experienced trauma.

Another inexpensive way to get counseling is by calling the universities in your area and asking if they have a student internship clinic that provides free mental health services for the community. Some universities have their master's students run clinics that provide one-to-one sessions and groups for free. The counselors you will see during these types of sessions are master's level interns who are being supervised by expert faculty who observe the therapy sessions over closed-circuit cameras or two-way mirrors. Don't worry—the faculty are not watching you, they are watching their students. And you should be aware that these students are likely to be cautious, since they are still learning. If you want to explore this option, you should look for universities that have the following types of programs: Master of Education, Psychology, Social Work, or Counseling programs. A bonus tip is to look for universities that have accreditation through CACREP (Council for Accreditation of Counseling & Related Educational Programs). This accreditation ensures that the university adheres to strict national standards for providing mental health services.

In addition to these options, some mental health agencies have sliding fee scales, because they offer therapy sessions with interns or associate level providers. For example, a master's level student intern may charge $25 per session, an associate counselor (who has already graduated from a master's program) may charge $65, and an independent provider may charge $125 per session. Remember these providers are at different levels of practice, so you may need to seek out another provider, if you do not feel supported or heard by your counselor.

How Can I Find a Therapist?

The website *Psychology Today* is a trusted and powerful tool. It can help you search providers in many ways:

- by age
- by gender
- by insurance
- by language

- by price
- by types of service
- by zip code

The site can even help you search for support groups. This website verifies that the provider is state licensed and in good standing. After you complete your searches and feel that you have found the right providers—they have the right letters after their name and they accept your health insurance—then, there's only one thing left to do: trust your gut! You will know.

When you meet someone for the intake, ask yourself these questions:

- Are they listening?
- Are they being dismissive?
- Are their answers too simple for my life?
- Are they talking too much about themselves?
- Do I feel safe here?
- Do I want to tell my story to this person?
- Can this person hear my pain?

One important note: I do not recommend asking a friend for the name of their therapist. Your needs are likely different than your friend's. Do your own research, meet with your provider, and if it doesn't feel right, find a new one!

If I Am on Medication, Do I Need Therapy?

Millions of people use medication to help with sleep, anxiety, and depression. It is beyond the scope of this book to cover the topic of psychotropics. (Be sure to read my concerns about these medications in chapter three under "Psychotropics," and in chapter five under "Oversimplification in Mental Health.") However, I will share my personal opinion: medications work best when they are used in combination with mental health treatment. Throwing medication at a symptom without addressing underlying issues is not going to solve the problem over the long term—it is just a quick fix. It is like taking aspirin for a headache when you actually need to drink more water. Medication can help, but for long-term results, you need to get to the root of the problem through talk therapy. Try both instead of relying on just one or the other. During my years of practice, I have heard clients say, "I've got this. I take happy pills." My response is always the same, "Wouldn't it be awesome to also look at why you need happy pills in the first place?"

Is This Confidential?

Confidentiality is foundational in mental health therapy. A client should feel safe as they talk about their issues and their lives, and that their therapist is protecting their information. Before you begin treatment, every therapist should have you sign a confidentiality and informed consent form. The form should state that your therapist will not share anything from your session with anyone else without your written consent. Moreover, it is illegal and unethical for a therapist to release any information, written or verbal, without a signed consent form from the client. A therapist cannot share information about you with your spouse or other family members. The therapist cannot even acknowledge that you attend therapy without obtaining your written permission. If you do want a family member, your doctor, or your attorney to have access to your records, you will need to sign a release of information form.

You should be aware that there are exceptions. Most therapists are mandated by the state to report these areas of concern:

- child abuse
- elder abuse
- exploitation of disabled persons
- harm to self or harm to others
- parental neglect
- sex abuse

Your counselor may have agreed to requirements outlined by a court (when court-ordered therapy is mandated) and your insurance provider. For example, most insurance companies require therapists to disclose a client's diagnosis. In addition, there are other times when a therapist cannot uphold client confidentiality. For example, in Arizona, people under the age of eighteen have no confidentiality when it comes to a therapist sharing information with their legal guardians. (I think this is unfortunate, because sharing information with legal guardians can sometimes be detrimental to the goals of therapy and cause a child to withhold important information from their therapist.) I always tell teenagers that a custodial parent could ask for their records at any time. You should check about the limits of confidentiality in your state.

What Happens in a Therapy Session?

Your first therapy session will probably be non-eventful. You will likely fill out some paperwork, which will go into a chart that your therapist will keep. Some charts contain paper records, and some are kept electronically. The chart will contain the forms that a particular state requires. Most charts will have an intake form, which is a general overview of your history and your concerns. You will also fill out an informed consent form, which outlines your confidentiality and the limits to that confidentiality. There may be other forms that cover your history in more detail, a mental health evaluation, and a mental status intake form. Your therapist uses these forms to screen for abnormalities, to assess whether you are a danger to yourself or to others, and to see if you are a victim of domestic violence. Your therapist might also ask you to participate in an initial assessment, like the Beck Depression Inventory, the Michigan Alcohol Screening Test (MAST), or the Substance Abuse Subtle Screening Inventory (SASSI).

One important note: your first session may be a longer session, and it may cost more than a regular session, but these factors should be clearly explained to you up-front. Your therapist should also let you know how billing will work and how much each session will cost. In addition, you should take some time during this first session to see if you can get a sense of your therapist's personality and willingness to hear you.

During the first or second session, you will also complete a treatment plan with your therapist. The purpose of a treatment plan is to outline why you are seeking counseling. Your therapist will likely ask you something like, "What do you want to work on?", and you will probably set some short- and long-term goals. Remember, these goals should have meaning for you! They should also be reviewed every few months, as your needs will likely change, if your life does.

Also remember that your therapist may be required to share your treatment plan and your diagnosis with your insurance provider. You should be aware of this at the outset, so please ask your therapist what they share with the insurance company.

Treatment plans shouldn't be complicated or hard to understand. Here are some examples:

- To treat anxiety, your plan could include increasing your awareness of anxiety triggers or decreasing your negative coping strategies that relate to anxiety.
- To treat depression, your plan could include creating a safety plan, increasing your self-awareness about depression, increasing positive coping strategies, decreasing negative coping strategies, and exploring your history, behavior, and causes of depression.
- To treat substance abuse, your plan could include decreasing your use, increasing your awareness of the thoughts you have before and after use, decreasing negative coping strategies, and decreasing a specific behavior (such as fighting every time you drink).

As you can see, your treatment plan is in direct alignment with your diagnosis. Your treatment plan outlines specific goals that you will work toward to provide relief. (See the next section, "What Is a Diagnosis?", for more information.)

After your first and second sessions, therapy becomes a conversation between you and your therapist. You will spend your time talking, learning, and practicing tools or skills. Your counselor will use therapeutic techniques to help you sort through your issues. You may get homework from your therapist and report back on how the week went. Don't worry if you don't complete the homework; go ahead and attend the session anyway. Your therapist will understand and maybe you can explore or practice the technique in the session. Do not be afraid to ask questions or get clarification.

What Is a Diagnosis?

A diagnosis is a label given to you to identify the behavioral symptoms that you are reporting. This label comes from a book called the *Diagnostic and Statistical Manual of Mental Disorders* (the DSM). Your provider gives you a diagnosis based on your presentation in the first and second session. Your therapist is looking for specific behaviors and symptoms listed in the DSM.

In the early 1900s, many university labs would create lists to code problem mental health behaviors, until 1952 when the American Psychiatric Association published the first *Diagnostic and Statistical Manual: Mental Disorders* (DSM-I). This text became the principal tool for psychiatric diagnoses. But the DSM was not universally welcomed. The DSM was and is criticized because of its poor validity and reliability. A common critique is that different clinicians give different diagnoses to the same client. In addition, therapists noted that a diagnosis can change for a client over time, and the DSM does not account for this. Finally, some criticized it as being a "disease model," giving clients a negative, long-lasting label.

Though the DSM has been updated many times (versions include DSM-II, DSM-III, DSM-IV, DSM-TR, DSM-5), the text still focuses on problem behavior and mental disease, instead of mental health. Regardless, the insurance companies use the DSM coding system to determine what types of treatment they will fund. Most therapists, psychologists, and psychiatrists use the DSM today for insurance and billing. They all must be able to speak the language of the DSM to advocate for their clients, so the insurance companies will approve the appropriate number of therapy sessions. As a client, you should be aware of the pros and cons of receiving a documented diagnosis. Your therapist can discuss this with you. Common diagnoses include mood disorders (depression) or anxiety.

If you have been diagnosed in the past, this may not matter. Many times, a past diagnosis is no longer relevant. A diagnosis is usually made within the first twenty-four hours after an intake. How can anyone summarize you after just one or two sessions? Remember your old diagnosis was made by one clinician, at one point in time, taking a snapshot of your behavior. A diagnosis is not who you are! A diagnosis is simply a listing of behaviors that the clinician saw at your intake. You don't need to be attached to a label. You are much more than a collection of behaviors.

CHAPTER SEVEN

COMMON TYPES OF TREATMENT

Jenny, it has been a long time since we met, but I need you again. My current therapist told me to pretend my brother was sitting in the chair next to me and talk to him. It felt weird at first, but then I began to cry, and all of my frustration came out about his life, him abandoning the family, and his years of bad choices. Mom cries every night about him. She wails something in Italian, spits, and wrings her hands. I guess the therapy is working. My head felt much lighter when I left. I felt more peaceful. I guess if my brother isn't around, "the chair thing" works. She called it "empty chair." She seems nice, but is this a normal counseling technique? Should I keep trying this out? (Letter from a former client)

A research study[1] was conducted several years ago that looked at all the different types of mental health treatment and tried to summarize what really works in therapy. The investigators

---

[1] Sprenkle, Douglas H, and Blow, Adrian J. (2004). "Common factors and our sacred models." *Journal of Marital & Family Therapy*, 30(2). 113-129.

examined 475 separate studies and concluded that it didn't matter what type of treatment the therapist used. In other words, the outcome of treatment did not change based on the technique the therapist used.

This study offers consumers a lot of wisdom. So, if psychological theory and therapist technique do not create change, what does? The study found that **the client felt better if they had a good relationship with their counselor.**[2] So, the most important thing for you to remember when considering therapy is not what type of treatment you should get. Instead, you should listen to your gut. Ask yourself, "Is this therapist listening to me? Do I feel safe sharing my story? Are they judging me? How do they support me?"

Given all of this research, you may wonder why it is important for you to understand what types of treatment are out there. In order for you to be an educated consumer, I think it's helpful to know the most common types of therapy. You should have a basic understanding of what are called "treatment modalities," because this understanding might give you some insight into a prospective therapist and the type of relationship you might expect to have with her.

As mentioned in previous chapters, you can visit the website for *Psychology Today* to find profiles of counselors. These profiles include information about what types of treatment modalities each counselor specializes in. Explore the site and read through the descriptions. What do your instincts tell you? If a particular type of treatment sounds good to you, check and see if there are therapists near you who specialize in this style. Remember, you

---

[2] Ibid.

should like your therapist and feel safe discussing your concerns, no matter what modality she uses!

Types of treatment are sometimes called *theories, treatment, treatment modalities, techniques, models, practice,* or *therapy.* Understanding these different theories will allow you to see a therapist's point of view. This lens is basically how the therapist works with you after the intake.

Behaviorism

Many psychologists are trained in behavioral techniques. Pure behaviorism focuses on the idea that all behavior is learned and can be unlearned. As a result, therapists who practice behaviorism use specific techniques to reinforce a change of behavior in their clients, by using rewards or punishments. (A common example is using a sticker chart when kids complete household chores.) Behaviorism is mainly used in substance-abuse treatment, parenting models, in classrooms, and in child therapy. The military also uses a behaviorism approach during boot camp.

CBT or Cognitive Behavioral Therapy

Cognitive Behavioral Therapy (CBT) is a very popular type of treatment. It focuses on a central idea: if you change your thoughts, you can change your behavior. Many therapists specialize in CBT and post it on their websites. During a session using CBT, you would be asked to, "Pick a value, behavior, or choice that you want to change." Once you say the answer, your therapist would ask, "What were you thinking just before you did the thing you want to change?" This will lead you down a path of exploring the thoughts that trigger the behavior you want to change. Your therapist will explore with you your belief systems (not religious beliefs) that you hold about yourself and others, to see if any hinder your wellbeing. You will also explore your "rational versus irrational" beliefs. (This means deciding what is a real belief versus what is your fear talking.)

This type of therapy often involves some form of homework, like journaling, and keeping track of your behaviors. Some therapists will give you tools for self-care or will focus on self-awareness (they will ask you to "notice when you are sad"). Some therapists will ask you to take action when you are experiencing an emotion: they will tell you to get involved, reach out to a friend, or volunteer. Other therapists might ask you to limit certain actions: stop watching the news, stop listening to talk radio as you drive, or stop calling your mother before bed. All of these techniques are based on the notion that changing your habitual behavior will change your thoughts or changing your thoughts will change your behavior.

Existentialism

The existentialist therapist believes that facing our death is crucial to living a full life. The therapist is a sort of philosopher questioning about how death informs our life. During sessions using this type of theory, you would explore your purpose, look at what has meaning in your life and what has no meaning, and discuss the point of our existence. This exploration would attempt to root you in your deeper purpose.

Family Therapy

Family therapy is usually offered by a Marriage and Family Therapist (MFT). The focus of this treatment is on the family as a group or system, not on the individual and their unique problems. These therapists usually request that all members of the family attend the sessions. This is a challenging treatment style if certain family members don't want to participate or if they blame a specific individual in the family for the problems. This work can be extremely valuable when the entire family comes together with the goal of healing unhealthy family dynamics.

Gestalt and Mindfulness-Based Practice

Gestalt is the work of psychiatrist Fritz Perls. His approach is focused on the "here and now." A Gestalt therapist would use a technique called "empty chair." In this practice you would speak to the empty chair, as if someone you wanted to talk to was sitting in it. The therapist might also ask you to participate in role reversal, where you behave and speak as someone else. Another technique is mindfulness, where you focus on each moment and stay present without your mind creating a story. This therapeutic style seeks to bring your focus from the past into the present moment.

Here's an example, if you had unfinished business with your deceased grandmother. The therapist might ask you to bring a photograph of her into one of your sessions, place it in a chair in front of you, and speak to the photograph as if it really was your grandmother sitting there. All of this work focuses on awareness and what is happening now in the present moment.

Many new mindfulness practices have been developed from Gestalt theory including the following "mindfulness" approaches:

- Mindfulness-Based Stress Reduction (MBSR)
- Mindfulness-Based Cognitive Therapy (MBCT)
- Acceptance and Commitment Therapy (ACT)
- Dialectical Behavior Therapy (DBT)

Person-Centered Work

Person-centered or client-centered work focuses on the client. Technically, every therapist should be client-centered to some degree, but a person-centered therapist focuses primarily on relationship building above all other goals. Instead of directing the therapy sessions, a person-centered therapist will allow the client to set the pace and discuss the topics of their choice. These therapists will validate you and give you a safe non-judgmental place to cry, grieve, be angry, or sort out ideas. Some clients in a person-centered session may feel frustrated and want more direction from the therapist. Person-centered therapists serve as a mirror, reflecting back to the client, instead of offering suggestions.

Psychoanalytic or Psychodynamic Theory

Psychoanalytic Theory, Analysis, or Psychodynamic Theory are all the same concept. This approach was developed by Sigmund Freud, Alfred Adler, and Carl Jung, and it focuses on the early parts (birth until age eight) of an individual's life. This method of therapy emphasizes early childhood experiences to determine whether these early experiences relate to current problems in your life. For example, if you are having trouble with a power dynamic at work and you tell the therapist that your dad was an overbearing figure, the therapist would connect the present stress to the past stress. Psychoanalytic therapists will often explore your defense mechanisms, interpret your dreams, examine your experiences at different stages in your development, look at how your birth order in the family has shaped you, and dig deep into formative experiences that took place in your early childhood.

Reality Theory

Probably the most famous reality therapist today is Dr. Philip C. McGraw, commonly known as Dr. Phil. You may be familiar with this TV personality who often asks, "How's that working for you?" That question is typical for these types of therapists. Reality therapists will ask you to take inventory of your behaviors, set goals, and take responsibility for your actions. Many substance-abuse counselors use this modality, as it is very similar to Alcoholics Anonymous and other twelve-step programs. This type of therapy tends to be a bit more direct and confrontational than others. If you participate in this type of therapy, be ready to take responsibility for your behaviors.

Populations

So far in this book, we've categorized therapists by what degrees they have earned (the letters that appear after their names) and what treatment modalities they specialize in. There's also one other factor to consider when trying to find the right therapist for you: what population groups they specialize in. For example, I specialize in children ages one to eighteen and in adults suffering from the effects of childhood trauma. Other populations include these:

- aging adults
- athletes
- children
- first responders
- gang members
- incarcerated individuals
- indigenous peoples

- infants
- LGBTQIA+ individuals
- people needing career guidance
- people of faith
- people suffering with grief and loss
- people who are homeless
- people who have sexual struggles
- people with addictions
- people with disabilities
- specific racial or ethnic groups
- teens
- veterans
- victims of crime

If you've read these first seven chapters, I hope it's clear how many things you'll want to consider before choosing your therapist. Take the time to study a few different counselors until you find the right person who can help you with your specific concerns.

CHAPTER EIGHT

Couples Work

Once again, I need some advice. The past few months have been very difficult, along with the normal day-to-day stresses of business owning, home owning, and child rearing, we threw in that weird situation with the woman from Michael's past, and TODAY, the clearing and sale of his sister's home in Fort Collins. I'm sure I've shared that she is a hoarder. I took two weeks off from work, put my head down, and helped her sort. We are now about 90 percent done and the house is under sales contract. I have so many concerns, and Michael is not in a space (emotionally, mentally) to really listen to any of them. Through this process, his own hoarding habits have been pushed up. He becomes very defensive at the slightest thing, and more and more items from his sister's house are finding their way here, to our already full house. I have found myself silent much of the time, because speaking up never goes well. Last night he yelled at me, "You don't have an f-ing clue." I know he's frustrated with his sister, but he hasn't expressed anything to her. Instead he has become like a time bomb at home, especially with the kids and me. I feel myself literally shrinking away. I have lost sixteen pounds. (I needed to) but the act of shrinking has also been on purpose, and I am panicking over my future! Michael is working full time now, so he does not have to deal with his sister during this time. Again, it all falls on me. So, I feel it is important that I get in to speak to someone professionally and gain some new tools that I don't currently have. I would love for Michael to join me, but I have asked him before and he has said no, stating that he doesn't "believe in quacks." So many roadblocks. Sigh. I'm wondering who or what method of therapy you would suggest (Letter from a former client)

Couples Work Requires an Expert

Couples work is a very challenging type of therapeutic work, and it requires a therapist who has specialized training. Most associate level counselors (interns and new graduates) do not have enough training or knowledge about the theory and practice of couples work to help. In fact, most beginning counselors fall into the trap of facilitating a couple's session like an individual session.

Couples work needs to address the deeper layers of the conflict (the emotion and the history). No progress can be made when the couple stays in a place where they are arguing about injustices and trading insults. A good therapist can shift a couples perspective to a higher quality of communication and life, helping the couple work through unresolved emotions.

If you are trying to find a therapist who works with couples and you are reviewing therapist profiles on the website for *Psychology Today*, look for someone with many years of experience (at least five years) who lists treatment modalities with names like

Imago, Gottman, or other couples training. You want a therapist who can see the couple as a whole, not as two individuals.

A couples counselor needs to have specialized training in recognizing and addressing domestic violence, and the cycle of power and control.

The truth about couples work is that each person in the relationship could also benefit from individual sessions prior to attending couples therapy. Couples therapy works best when each person in the relationship already has some clarity about what they want, they have vented their frustrations, and set their personal boundaries BEFORE coming in to couples work. To save yourself time and money, schedule couples work after you know yourself and your own needs better. (You can visit the website for the Gottman Institute to learn more about couples work.)

Partner Violence

Intimate partner violence is known as domestic violence (DV). It is a terrible statistic to contemplate, but one half of all women in the United States have suffered from at least one form of DV from their partner – verbal, physical, sexual, or mental. It is important to note at the outset that DV does not have to include physical abuse. Most women assume that, if her partner is not hitting her, she is not a victim of DV. DV can happen when someone exerts abusive power and control over their partner's finances, jobs, friendships, weekend activities, social time, parenting of children, or in other areas. And women are not the only victims of DV. While the number of men who report partner violence is lower than women, we know many men do not report it.

Unfortunately, we know that incidents of DV can escalate and sometimes lead to a partner's death. DV is cyclical in nature—a partner can be angry and aggressive at times, and then show love, apologize, and give gifts. If you question whether you are living in an abusive relationship, a good place to begin your investigation is to track your partner's cycles. Do they display a repeated cycle that moves from irritability to anger and then an apology? Always trust your instincts. Be cautious and get out of relationships where you sense there is too much jealousy and control. Safety is your first concern! Make sure your car, home, credit cards, and bank accounts are in your name. Create a back-up plan, in case you need to leave your home quickly. Store important documents at a trusted friend's home.

Educate yourself about abuse and the options you have to address it. Find a therapist to work with you who is open, honest, and educated about DV. Here are two good resources:

- National Sexual Assault Hotline: RAINN: 1-800-656-HOPE (4673)
- National Domestic Violence line at 1-800-799-7233

CHAPTER NINE

CRISIS AND TRAUMA

I am so scared of him. He plays video games twelve hours a day. He drives 120 miles per hour down the freeway. He drinks and drives!!!! He wrapped his car around a sign! Then he talked the cops into driving him home. He was drunk, I have no idea how he got out of a ticket with that mess. Do you know, he gets so angry that he tears up the tile in the bathroom? He destroyed his microwave, he pulled the door off its hinges! He totally scares me. Sometimes I pretend that I am not home when he comes over at night. His aggression is so scary. I think he is trying to kill himself. I called his mom the other day, just to feel like I wasn't living this alone. (Letter from a former client)

I include crisis and trauma in this book due to the fact that so many people are affected by trauma. You may be reading this book because you are concerned about a loved one or you may be struggling with a crisis yourself. An estimated 70 percent of adults in the United States have experienced a traumatic event at least once in their lives. We should be aware of the warning signs of suicide. I believe that we are a community that cares about each other, and therefore, we should notice people in distress and direct them to the right support system.

Crisis

What are the warning signs for suicide? Suicidal people usually do not see another way out. They are missing the tool in their tool box that will help them brainstorm alternatives. They do not want this life right now. They are stuck in this moment, this future, this now, and they see the present circumstances as permanent. They see no other future. When they turn to suicide, they are not seeking attention. They are seeking relief.

Addressing suicidal thoughts and behaviors can be quite challenging. Sometimes talk therapy helps. Speaking with a nonjudgmental person about feelings of frustration, being stuck in a life they don't want to live, can have a calming effect. A therapist might even brainstorm with their client about alternative choices. If you fear that someone you love is suicidal, it's important to understand that talking to a person about suicide will not make the suicidal person kill themselves.

Someone who is suicidal often displays some of the following common warning signs:

- Abusing drugs or alcohol
- Acting impulsively
- Acting recklessly
- Appearing depressed or sad most of the time (untreated depression is the number one cause for suicide)
- Behaving impulsively

- Changing eating habits
- Changing sleeping habits
- Exhibiting a change in personality
- Experiencing dramatic mood changes
- Feeling excessive guilt or shame
- Feeling helpless
- Feeling hopeless
- Feeling intense anger or rage
- Feeling trapped, as though there is no way out of a situation
- Giving away prized possessions
- Losing interest in most activities
- Performing poorly at work or in school
- Talking or writing about death or suicide
- Withdrawing from family and friends
- Writing a will

It should be noted that some people who die by suicide do not show any suicidal warning signs. But about 75 percent of those who die by suicide do exhibit some suicidal warning signs, so it is important to stay aware and try to spot them. Also, do not neglect, ignore, or provoke a suicidal person. Extend compassion to the person and seek help from a professional. If you do know someone who exhibits suicidal warning signs, do everything you can to help them. If a loved one has some of the symptoms above and you are wondering what to do, first, think about their safety. If you aren't sure, but suspect someone is having suicidal thoughts, ask them. They may respond with anger, but angry is better than dead.

There are many places to reach out for help:

- National Suicide Prevention Lifeline at 800.273.TALK (8255)
- Crisis Text Line by texting HOME to 741741
- Suicide: Read this first.
- SAMHSA, Suicide Prevention Resources
- Trans Lifeline: (877) 565-8860

Trauma

I have no money, but I spent 210 dollars on eyelashes. I wanted to feel pretty. Sam made me mad for four days now. He told me that after having sex with his porn star twenty-year-old, he said sex with regular women was ruined forever. I got very mad and called him on it. He is using "porn logic" and objectifying women. Men are encouraged to masturbate, and condoms are thrown at them. Girls are told to zip it up. Don't look, don't touch, or you are a slut and don't be a slut. Women need to be taught about their bodies and orgasms. If Sam has found a porn star, okay, but I bet she has also had sexual trauma in her life! He is forty-five years old, she is twenty, that is gross! I have an idea, don't objectify her and further her trauma. Screw him. He has been a self-absorbed jerk. He is detoxing off an eight-week steroid detox and he is a raving lunatic. I want to say good bye, but I am hurt. He is immature, self-serving, childlike, and narcissistic. When I moved out, he didn't care. He never asked me to come back. He didn't even get off the couch. Why do I care who he dates? I care because I do. I can't tell if this is my old trauma from when I was raped in high school

> *or if this is me with correct feelings. I am all messed up. How do I even trust men or date ever again? I have no idea whether I am coming or going. I thought I'd dealt with all of this! (Letter from a former client)*

What is trauma? Trauma is our emotional reaction to a disturbing event. After a traumatic event, we are thrown into a chaotic, stressed state, feeling overwhelmed with emotions. We feel helpless as our mind struggles to make sense of an event that we cannot figure out. How can we make sense of a sudden death, a fire, a mass shooting, or a violent attack? We try anyway. We seek to understand our circumstances, because we believe that understanding will help us survive. We look out at the world that harmed us and we seek feedback from our surroundings. Our mind reviews the details day and night to arrive at an understanding, but the event doesn't make sense. This is why trauma is a repetitive cycle—we are constantly reviewing and rewinding the event. This is extremely frustrating and so our mind, in an effort to be helpful, creates a story. The story that we create about our trauma can limit us or empower us. The helpful story can support us as we avoid risk and stay safe. Like a lesson, it says to us, "Remember this!" Trauma also causes us to tell ourselves *unhelpful* stories, creating unhelpful beliefs such as these:

- "All men are rapists."
- "Avoid grocery stores."
- "Don't trust people."
- "I am a failure."
- "I am bad."
- "I am broken."

- "I am different."
- "I am invisible."
- "I am not good enough."
- "I am not smart enough."
- "I am worthless."
- "I will never love anyone again."
- "If gain weight I won't be attractive to men."
- "No one believes me."

The stories we tell ourselves become maps; they help us navigate and look for danger. These stories were once just thoughts that passed through our heads. Now, after the trauma, they have become beliefs that inform our lives. They serve as a lens through which we see the world, our GPS system with which we navigate our course. They are "avoidance thoughts," telling us to turn left, right, retreat, or move forward. These unhelpful beliefs create limits, make us feel stuck, and cause us to create repetitive patterns.

What does this tell us about trauma? The pain we experience isn't all due to the traumatic event itself. Some of the pain comes from the story that we tell ourselves about what happened. I want to emphasize that even though I am using the terms *stories* and *beliefs*, I am not downplaying real pain. These trauma stories can influence all aspects of our physical, mental, and emotional well-being. Trauma reactions are real and can negatively impact our job, our relationships, our health, and our daily functioning. I hope to illustrate that our mind creates coping strategies without our mental awareness. These stories are happening under the surface.

Memory and Trauma

Memory is tricky after a trauma. When trauma happens, we remember things in a complicated way, attempting to understand the unbelievable thing that happened to us. We focus on some aspects of the trauma and ignore others. Sometimes we remember false details—events that simply didn't happen. Other details we block and choose to not think about at all. If we don't remember all of the actual details, our brains will fill in the blanks to help us make sense of what happened. So, in effect, our brains lie to us to protect us. False or real, the memories we relive and replay in our minds are the ones that become stronger.

I will share an example. I work with kids who often speak about their parents physically fighting. The kids hear raised voices and slamming doors, but they don't actually see anything. The fight is happening in another room. But their minds fill in the blanks. Without seeing any visual evidence, they imagine that their parents are physically harming each other. In reality, the parents could be arguing without any physical contact. (*Side note: This verbal abuse is domestic violence and can create post-traumatic stress disorder (PTSD) as easily as seeing physical harm being inflicted.*)

The brain fills in missing details because it needs to stay safe. The brain says, "I must live." We are biologically wired with a drive to survive. It may not make sense that the brain is "protecting" us by telling us that our parents are physically fighting. However, if we think Mom and Dad are hurting each other, we will prepare to leave or fight. So, the mind searches its history, reviews past events, and adjusts its behavior to reduce risk. The child may be in their room packing to leave or getting ready to battle. These survival instincts kick in quickly to protect us.

We each have different coping mechanisms to respond to danger—sometimes we confront the danger (fight), sometimes we run away (flight), and sometimes we can't do anything (freeze). This is why bad memories are easier to remember than good ones. The brain wants us to remember the bad memories as warning signs to avoid danger.

Additionally, memories "live" all over the brain. When we recall something, the memory is reassembled from little pieces. Emotions help us recall memories faster. For example, painful memories or exciting thoughts can reassemble more quickly and they are the more prominent memories. Memories of stressful times are easy to remember: the pain is right on the surface; it takes only a small trigger to remember the bad event. The mind, body, and senses store trauma. Even a smell may trigger memories and feelings of past trauma. In fact, smell is the strongest trigger for resurfacing trauma.

Behavior and Trauma

Unfortunately, time does not heal trauma. If we could ignore our past successfully, we would! But these unresolved issues come back to us in many ways, such as unhealthy behaviors or repeating worries.

There are several behaviors that are common indicators of trauma, and, unfortunately, trauma can often mimic other things, so it can be difficult to identify. Here are some examples:

- a bad memory
- a foggy mind
- a lack of focus
- a learning disability

- absent mindedness
- addictions
- an inability to concentrate
- an inability to respond to questions
- an inability to speak clearly
- anxiety
- attention seeking
- avoiding people during holidays or seasonal changes
- bargaining or negotiating in an effort to create safety
- confusion
- depression
- exhaustion
- experiencing a flood of strong emotions
- feeling a lack of control
- feeling disconnected from conversations
- hypervigilance
- impaired thoughts
- money issues
- over-intellectualization
- self-blame
- sexualized behaviors
- shutting down
- staring off
- startle response
- trying to be perfect

Traumatized people are filled with anger, fear, self-doubt, and helplessness. They see the world as unpredictable and hostile. They may show a limited trust of themselves, others, or their environment. Most traumatized people have poor communication skills and an inability to verbally express their needs, especially about the trauma. Their behavior stems from many causes, including a perceived powerlessness to affect their future. In addition, they may release their emotions as fear, hostility, depression, or disorganized chaos.

After a scary, traumatic experience, we might "read" trauma into neutral events. Sometimes we can't even tell if we are really in danger. But our minds and our bodies respond in the same way, whether we are really in danger or whether the danger is only perceived. For example, we will avoid a restaurant where we acquired a food-borne illness. The restaurant is neutral, but our upset stomach was real. We may have a real fear of something, like a fear of getting married after listening to our parents' fight. We can also feel a sense of "futurelessness." We may not make preparations to buy a house, have children, or engage in long-term planning. We may have repetitive nightmares or flashbacks as our mind tries to make sense of the why.

If trauma repeats over and over again in our lives, the more likely we are to "disassociate" from our bodies. The idea of disassociation is difficult to describe, but it's a sense that you leave your body, that you and your body are separate. For example, if your father were an alcoholic, you may start to "disappear" from your thoughts and body when you hear his truck pull in the driveway. You prepare yourself in advance for the upcoming trauma. Remembering past trauma can also make us feel frozen in time. We may feel an old emotional charge related to something in the past; it's as if we are back in our childhood classroom, experiencing the trauma all over again.

Most therapists can help provide coping strategies for the after-effects of trauma, but you need a specialist to *heal* the trauma.

Here are the types of treatment that heal trauma:

- Eye Movement Desensitization and Reprocessing (EMDR)
- Emotional Freedom Technique (EFT)
- Brain Spotting
- Somatic Experiencing

What Is EMDR?

My favorite trauma work is Eye Movement Desensitization and Reprocessing, also known as EMDR. I want to take a moment to describe it, because it works! And it is faster than other methods. I have been practicing EMDR since 2000. I have seen hundreds of children and adults get relief from nightmares and repetitive thoughts. One of the great advantages of EMDR is that relief is faster than traditional talk therapy. The EMDR Institute states, "repeated controlled studies have shown that a single trauma can be processed within 3 sessions in 80-90% of the participants."

EMDR has been proven to effectively resolve trauma and negative self-beliefs. It focuses on the unresolved emotion and the unprocessed past event. In effect, EMDR removes the old emotional charge connected to that memory. The memory of the event does not go away, but the emotional charge associated with it disappears. The process and the equipment used in an EMDR session are not intrusive.

EMDR is not used to retrieve forgotten or unknown memories. Instead, it changes our current emotional response to the memories that are problematic. EMDR can be used with people of all ages and, because there is no overreliance on talking or language, it can be used across language barriers. A client participating in EMDR does not have to reveal their thoughts, and there is no homework.

What Happens During the First EMDR Session?
During the first intake session, you will fill out paperwork, review your history, and discuss behaviors that upset you. Your therapist may ask you to complete a trauma timeline, which is a more detailed history of your traumatic experiences. The therapist will explain what EMDR is, work with you to set your personal goals, ask how frequently you would like to have your sessions, and schedule your next appointment.

How Many Sessions Will EMDR Take?
EMDR is considered a more effective treatment modality than other types of trauma treatments, because it usually produces rapid and effective change. Most sessions are scheduled one week apart, and most people attend three to seven sessions. Your therapist will monitor your progress and gauge how many sessions you may need. In order to practice EMDR, a therapist will need to take specialty training, so EMDR can sometimes cost more than talk therapy. But, again, it will require fewer sessions. The EMDR institute states that, "While every disturbing event need not be processed, the amount of therapy will depend upon the complexity of the history."

Many people who have experienced EMDR say that the process feels like ripping off a band aid. But you shouldn't worry that you will be asked to re-live traumatic events from your past or talk about the details of these events. Your therapist will ask you to focus on one visual image of the trauma. You may experience some intense emotions or sensations, but they usually last only a few minutes and then they will decrease in intensity. EMDR therapists are trained to help decrease the intensity of these feelings and relieve the distress.

You will leave the session feeling less upset and overwhelmed. Many clients report feeling calm, experiencing freedom from thoughts, or having reduced tension in their bodies. It is normal for memories to surface after an EMDR session; your brain is reprocessing the trauma! Before you leave the session ask the therapist about what you should do if you have a distressing memory. Some people find it is helpful to keep a journal of their thoughts during this treatment.

CHAPTER TEN

CHILDREN

Hey, I hope all is well. I have a few questions for you, if you don't mind. Xander has started his third year in Montessori. He has been three years at this school but this year he has a new teacher. Things have gotten pretty frustrating and I admit it is bringing up some old emotions for me. Xander has been accused of bullying and being intense with other kids. He often gets "red lights" at school. I have noticed that his anxiety has been a bit high. I am worried the school will ask us to leave. We could use a little advice. Tom and I seem to be on two different pages and although we are talking through it, we could use a little advice on how to proceed. Tom feels comfortable with me asking you a couple of questions and for that we seem to be in agreement. Do you think you can spare some time to talk in the next few days? We are really trying to decide if we need to bring in a therapist or if this is just normal kid stuff. (Letter from a former client)

Just like adults, children can benefit from a safe, neutral place to explore their feelings. When you look for a therapist, you should look for someone who has toys in her office, because that is a good indicator that the therapist uses a technique called play therapy. Play therapy is different than adult talk therapy. A therapist who uses play therapy will have an office full of games, toys, dollhouses, puppets, costumes for dress-up, a kitchen, miniature figurines, and art supplies. If you don't see any of these things, ask if there is a play therapy space in the office. If there isn't a designated space with toys, find a different provider. You should also ask the therapist about their training in working with children and specifically in play, art, or sand therapy (described in chapter three and below). They should be able to tell you about their specialized training. Trust your instincts here and ask yourself, "Is this therapist going to act as my child's advocate, or are they just interested in diagnosing my child?" I strongly recommend shopping around and find someone your child bonds with.

But there is an important step to take before you send your child to treatment. It is a good idea to first examine your definition of childhood. What are the behaviors that you expect from your child? What is developmentally appropriate? How does your child express emotions? How do you influence your child's behavior? Sometimes child therapy involves parenting and family involvement. It is good to have clarity about your child's behaviors before you bring your child in. Similar to a medical appointment, most child therapists will want to hear about the history of the behaviors and what makes the child's behavior improve or get worse.

Unfortunately, in the early days of child psychology, some misguided thinking became the foundation of the profession. The original goal of child psychology was to control and reduce child *mis*behavior. This theory of behaviorism became the underpinning philosophy in the field of child therapy, and because of it, children were seen as a set of behaviors that needed to be changed. A child's emotions and feelings were often left out. It is a way of thinking that still exists in the field of mental health today. It can even be seen in the educational system, as school psychologists and teachers set specific behavioral goals for your child. This is a limiting, narrow view of the experience of childhood. We owe our children the right to be seen as full humans with emotions and complex feelings.

In my opinion, a good child therapist should get to know the child first, trying to understand your child's feelings and thoughts to see if she can determine the root causes for any unhealthy behaviors. If a therapist simply tries to reduce behavior, the root anxiety, stress, or depression will still exist, and the behavior will change into another problem behavior. For example, if we ask the child to stop picking their fingers and put gloves on the child, the anxiety might move into their feet and they will begin kicking the chair in front of them. It is most beneficial to address the root of the anxiety instead of simply moving the behavior. In fact, when therapists address a root emotional cause, sometimes the problem behaviors immediately disappear. As a side note: feelings of powerlessness are often a root cause for a child's misbehavior, so you should seek a child therapist who sees and empowers your child.

The Process

You should expect a therapist to take a lengthy developmental history when your child begins treatment. You will be asked to participate in the intake session to provide information about any problems during pregnancy, the child's developmental milestones, peer relationships, preschool and school functioning, play activities, medical issues, and the family situation. You will also be asked who else lives in the house with you and your child.

Once the therapy sessions begin, your child's therapist will use play, art, and music therapy. These types of therapeutic techniques are important because children often use a "language" that does not involve words. Children communicate through play—it is their language. Play gives children a way to release stress and blow off tension and steam. Play gives them a way to achieve mastery, grow, discover rules, engage in sharing, learn to cooperate, take turns, and learn how to act in a group or outside of a group. A child will use play to deal with their feelings, their fears, their pain. In play, a child is saying, "Let me use my energy and symbols to work through my pain." Many therapists will involve family members in the therapy either before, after, or during the child's sessions.

As a side note: if your child's school or a court requires your child to attend therapy, make sure you ask your therapist if they will write the necessary court documents. The therapist may need extra training, extra time, and extra fees for such activities.

In terms of confidentiality, as described earlier in this book, each state has its own laws that govern what a therapist may say about your child and to whom. In the state of Arizona, for example, a child under the age of eighteen has no confidentiality. A legal parent or guardian can request charts, tests, and medical information from a health or mental health provider. I recommend looking into your state regulations regarding the rights of a minor child and limits of confidentiality. You do not want to promise your child that therapy is a safe space, if another guardian (such as your wife, husband, ex-husband, etc.) can legally obtain information about your child from the therapist.

Diagnosing Your Child

Your therapist should have a strong understanding of childhood development, especially when it comes to diagnosing your child. In order to define abnormal childhood behavior, a therapist must first have a deep understanding of normal development in children. It might be helpful to ask your therapist about what behaviors are normal for a child at a particular age or stage. It is also important to note that most children do not receive a specific diagnosis from their therapist. Instead, therapists most often treat children to relieve a symptom that came about from a major change in life: a loss, a divorce, a new problem behavior, a move to a new home, a change in school, or a trauma. There are a few childhood diagnoses, but keep in mind, these diagnoses are the exception to the rule. Often children are over diagnosed. Also remember that a diagnosis is simply a label of behaviors that the therapist sees during intake, this diagnosis may not follow the child into adulthood. Below are some common diagnoses.

Attention Deficit Hyperactivity Disorder

Attention deficit hyperactivity disorder (ADHD) is a term used for children who are unable to concentrate on a task for an appropriate period of time. Children with ADHD may also be observed fidgeting or impulsively talking. Some therapists will refer children with ADHD to doctors who prescribe stimulant drugs such as methylphenidate (Ritalin), to reduce disruptive behavior and improve concentration. Therapy for ADHD may involve parent training (these are specific techniques given to a parent to help lessen the child reactions) and creating classroom management techniques based on behavioral theory. These parent and school techniques will vary based on the child and the environment. To learn more about ADHD visit the websites for the Attention Deficit Disorder Association (ADDA) and the National Institute of Mental Health.

Conduct Disorder

Conduct Disorder (CD) is a diagnosis given to children who exhibit behaviors that violate the rights of others. This can include aggression and cruelty toward people or animals. Children with CD might damage property, lie, and steal. Children with CD often do not show remorse for what they have done, and it is more commonly diagnosed in boys. Treatment for children with CD often involves training parents to reward their child's positive behaviors. During the child therapy sessions, the child would work on anger control and behavior management. The therapist may seek to involve the school and probation officers, if beneficial for the child.

Reactive Attachment Disorder

Reactive Attachment Disorder (RAD) is a disorder that occurs during the first two years of a child's life when a child fails to attach or bond to a primary care giver. The child often appears standoffish or needy. The child may be detached from everyone and resist anyone's touch or nurturing. Or the child could inappropriately bond with strangers or lack appropriate boundaries with people they don't know.

Treatment with PCIT

The beginning of this chapter focuses on play therapy, but there is another wonderfully successful treatment style called Parent Child Interactive Therapy (PCIT), which was created for children who have experienced trauma, have CD or ADHD; any family can benefit from the work. Ideally, children between the ages of three and seven see the greatest benefits from PCIT. PCIT focuses on building a warm, positive relationship between parents and children, the goal is to increase positive coping skills and to decrease inappropriate behavior. This type of treatment requires active participation from the parents, and it takes place over a period of thirteen to sixteen weeks, with the therapist acting as the parents' coach. This treatment focuses on giving the parents tools to create a loving relationship with their child. To learn more about PCIT, visit the websites for PCIT International and the National Child Traumatic Stress Network.

Children and Sexual Trauma

If you suspect your child has been the victim of sexual assault or sexual misconduct, your first call needs to be to the police or the hospital for a forensic interview, which is a structured conversation or examination with a child intended to elicit detailed information about what the child may have experienced or witnessed. Some communities have specialized facilities and forensic specialists who conduct this type of interview. An officially trained forensic examiner—the person who conducts a forensic interview—will be able to provide you with documentation you may need in future court proceedings related to the assault or misconduct.

This is NOT a role for a therapist. Most therapists lack the specific type of training required in these types of situations. With the best of intentions, a therapist may innocently ask a child questions about their experience. This conversation could alter the child's perception and ultimately the child could change what they say occurred to them. As such, an interview with a therapist will not have the same weight in court as a forensic interview.

The time to look for a child therapist is AFTER the forensic interview has taken place. Therapy will eventually help a child process what has happened to them. Find a child therapist who specializes in sexual assault and children.

Parenting

Many people look to therapy as a way of finding guidance in parenting. If this is something you are seeking, I recommend finding a therapist who makes you smile, while giving you practical tools and strategies for parenting. Look for someone who has a sense of humor, is non-judgmental, and can provide concrete solutions.

As a side note, I want to include some parenting tips that I commonly share with clients:

- Apologize when you get it wrong. We can't be perfect parents, but we can be honest parents.
- Our children become what we do, not what we say.
- Ask questions about what went wrong before assigning blame or consequences.
- Be gentle with yourself, parenting is the hardest job that anyone can do!
- Competition is normal between and among siblings. Teach kindness and patience.
- Listen to your kids; they need a daily or weekly forum to vent their frustrations.
- Set clear expectations. Review the day in the morning and the evening.

- Spend one-on-one time with each of your children every day, even if it is only fifteen minutes a day by egg timer.
- Avoid "over-parentifying" your oldest children by expecting them to babysit or tutor younger children. Older children need to be kids, too.
- Teach your kids to be calm and peaceful.
- Life is not always fair. When it isn't fair, teach your child how to release their emotions safely. Give them a positive outlet like basketball to release anger.
- When you feel frustrated, engage in good self-care.

CHAPTER ELEVEN

GRIEF AND LOSS

I am just pretending that he is still here, but I haven't seen him. Can I just tell myself that he is on vacation? I hate it when people tell me that this happened for a reason or that he is in heaven looking down on me. I hate hearing that he was a good guy. I hate it all. I am not going to move on. I am not going to be peaceful with him being gone. This is hard to even talk about. I feel angry and numb. I feel pissed at my family as they are so full of church statements about God and guardian angels, blah, blah, blah. I am putting this in a box and placing it in the closet. I am not going to talk about it. I mean what is the worst thing that could happen? If I don't talk about it? I don't need to look at it. I'm not going to be helpless. I'm going to be angry instead. This isn't supposed to happen this way. I just will pretend he went on a business trip. (Letter from a former client)

Knowledge of oral traditions teaches us that, back in the days when humans lived in caves, a person who was grieving a loss would be left in the cave while the other members of the community took on the tasks of daily life: cooking, cleaning, hunting, and harvesting. The group dictated that the grieving person could not safely leave the cave. They knew that the grieving person would be upset and distracted, and they could easily become a victim to the environment because of their distraction. The grieving person could be eaten by a dire wolf, for example or a saber-toothed cat. The grieving person would stay safely in the cave, protected until they felt strong enough to integrate back into the tribe's daily routines. Today, in other parts of the world, people are expected to dress in black and mourn for an entire year.

By contrast, here in the United States, employers often require their staff to be back at work within a week of the death of a loved one! This is unfortunate. It is safe to say that three days is not enough to regain a sense of balance after suffering a major loss. Most people who lose a loved one begin to neglect their regular activities. They stop caring about eating, paying bills, or getting dressed. Some grieving people even have physical symptoms, like chest pain or difficulty breathing. They claim the grief sucks all the air out of their lungs. Others describe grief as hitting them in waves, over and over again. Yet, even with these symptoms, I suspect many of us happily return to work within a few days after experiencing a loss, because we use work as a distraction. We don't want to feel the pain.

Grief can occur after any type of loss: the death of a loved one, the end of a relationship, the death of a pet, the loss of a home, the end of a marriage or job, retirement, aging, empty nest syndrome, or after receiving a medical diagnosis. You can experience grief after losing anything you care about. Loss often makes us feel overwhelmed and out of control.

Grief has many faces. In other words, grief may express itself through many types of emotions or actions: anger, resistance, sadness, denial, frustration, guilt, shock, or fear. Grief is messy, chaotic, exhausting, distracting, causing us to cry, shake, or feel hatred. We may feel numb or overly sensitive. Sometimes it feels like we are crashing or grasping for anything normal. All of these emotions could be felt in one day!

There is nothing graceful about grief. Instead it causes unbearable pain and suffering. A grieving person can experience sudden bursts of crying, forgetfulness, or anger. As we grieve, our emotions are raw. We may show the world our worst self. Simple tasks can feel impossible. Answering questions, paying bills, getting dressed—they all seem impossible. Some people try to hold it all in and continue with their normal daily routine, attempting to block off their grief. This may work until one question, one song, one memory, one smell makes a crack in the dam, and we are flooded with emotions and pain.

Grief is undoubtedly the most unpleasant experience in the human catalogue. I always call grief the "gateway into therapy," because many people seek out counseling after a loss. People call a therapist because friends and family urge them to "go see someone." Friends and family feel powerless and helpless. It is hard for them to watch someone they love suffer. Well-meaning loved ones want to help the grieving person feel better. Yet, often in grief, nothing seems to help, nothing feels good. You feel lost and you don't know what you need. The truth is, grief is painful for everyone.

One of the reasons grieving people suffer so much is that our society does not teach us how to handle emotions. Most people are afraid of their emotions. I often hear my clients say in fear, "I will lose control." They feel vulnerable and anxious. What they are experiencing feels out of control. One minute, they feel fine, the next TV commercial triggers an emotional outburst. But feeling fragile, volatile, or unstable is normal when we grieve. Feeling out of control and feeling alone is normal, as well. Unfortunately, when our world is upside down, we cannot gauge what normal is.

You may have heard about the notion that we go through stages of grief. It's unfortunate that this theory has taken hold in popular culture, because experts who study grief tell us that these stages of grief do not describe the real-life process of grieving. The stages of grief are often too restrictive and narrow. Grief is a giant stewpot of bubbling emotions. If you're grieving, it's hard to anticipate when you'll next feel an intense emotion or why it is coming up.

Given all of this, it is important to understand that therapy doesn't "fix" grief. Grief is seen as a normal human experience. Therefore, therapy offers us a safe place to vent emotions. A grief counselor will encourage their client to express whatever is upsetting to them. The therapist will create a safe space and allow their client to process their feelings. This type of counseling guides the client to accept the new realities and adjust to the new normal, all while feeling the pain of the loss. A therapist will also counsel a grieving client to establish a support network, to perform self-care activities, and to find ways to make meaning out of the suffering. The therapist may discuss healthy coping strategies like engaging in a spiritual practice or philanthropy—things that give us a sense of purpose. The therapist may also explore concepts with their client about death, change, or impermanence.

Counseling advice to a grieving person is centered on self-kindness and allowing them to feel their feelings. If you are grieving, it is important to accept all of your emotions and overwhelming experiences with gentleness. Let yourself release your feelings. If you don't meet yourself with kindness, you'll only suffer more when you resist what is happening. Avoid statements like, "I should be over this by now." Remove the time limits. Suffering in life is unavoidable. Everyone's reactions to suffering differ. It will be easier if you do not judge yourself for what you feel or experience.

During the first weeks of the grieving process, resist making any major decisions. After a loss, avoid selling or buying a house or making drastic remodels to your life. Wait to get divorced or married. Wait to sell things of value. Avoid switching jobs. Wait to move. In the first few weeks, don't engage in major life decisions.

The good news is that grief eventually dissipates, and the pain lessens. Emotions will still come and go. You will get a blast of memory and burst out crying. Other days you will feel normal. Special occasions, holidays, anniversaries, or certain seasons can and may trigger a memory and sadness. Time doesn't really heal us. Instead, we learn to adapt to life without the person we've lost, without the kids in the house, and so on.

Time simply gives us distance. We don't move on, heal, or forget. We become shaped by our loss. We carry the loss forward with us into each new tomorrow. The hope is that we develop healthy coping strategies to deal with the pain.

When you are searching for a grief counselor, look for someone who appreciates the pain you are experiencing. Choose the counselor who makes you feel better and normalizes this experience for you. You will know when you feel seen and heard. As a side note: animals are great helpers during grief. They sense our loss and seem to know how to provide comfort.

CONCLUSION

BEING A GOOD CONSUMER

Anyone who feels that they have experienced some significant change in their life can benefit from therapy. Just make sure that you find someone who helps you feel calmer and more able to look at the difficult patterns in your life. When you start looking into therapy, evaluate it as you would any type of health service: research the provider, choose the right location that meets your needs, understand the costs up front, ask questions, and find a therapist that lets you become an equal partner in the process. Be clear with your therapist about your expectations or what you want from the experience. Then trust who you choose and let them do their best work.

You should never leave your first intake session with a new therapist saying something like, "I guess I have made bad decisions in my life. I felt like my new therapist was judging me." If you feel this way as you walk out the door, you are not seeing the right provider.

Before you attend the first intake session, do some self-examination and try to learn about yourself and the problems that are concerning you. For your first session, bring in a history of your problems and concerns. It is also helpful to share with your new therapist what techniques have worked for you in the past, as well as what hasn't worked. Do you have a self-care routine? How do you calm yourself down? The more details you can share with your new therapist at the intake session, the better your overall outcome will be in therapy.

Keep an open mind about the techniques of therapy. Even if they seem strange, many techniques that your therapist asks you to do are tested strategies and tools that will help you change your perspective. And, once you change your perspective, the world changes. The gift of therapy is that it allows us to look at our story, which in turn allows us to look at our relationship to fear. Don't be afraid of fear, because underneath all of that fear you will find love! Once we have experienced the fear, once we feel safe, love will emerge! I hope the therapist you find will allow you to feel safe.

Therapy, at its best, will empower you and give you a sense of balance and release, a feeling that you are reclaiming what is rightfully yours and creating space to experience your life and feel free.

If you were my client, I would say this to you:

You are not broken. You are not mentally ill. You are not crazy. You are a beautiful human. Your exhaustion is a common, human experience. We have each felt alone and overwhelmed. We have each needed nurturance and care. Can you rest, sleep, or let go of the plates that are spinning? Can you take time out to walk in nature or take a small break?

Remember the basics: manage your stress, eat well, get enough sleep, create a clean environment for yourself, drink lots of water, sit in the sunshine, have some fun, and sing! Don't forget the complementary practices of Chinese Reflexology, yoga, music, chiropractics, spiritual practices and community, and whatever form of creativity inspires you.

You don't have to know the answers. You can turn inward, ask yourself what you need, and begin to heal. Knowledge about yourself creates power. Your best self is a calm self, free from anxiety. Before we examine your patterns together, it would be helpful for you to nurture yourself. Get stronger before you begin to dig into exploring an old pattern. Allow the anger to come, write down your thoughts, and then see if you can shift to self-compassion.

There is nothing wrong with you. You are just feeling frustrated and unsteady. Emotions are healthy. Therapy is not about becoming perfect. We are all human, we all have issues. Life is about self-discovery and acceptance. Therapy helps people remember that they are acceptable just as they are! Show yourself kindness.

So, let's return to the title of this book, *Do I Need a Therapist?* You are the only one who knows that answer, but now you are full of knowledge and awareness to make a great decision for yourself! I wish you peace on your journey.

Referenced Websites

- American Art Therapy Association: https://arttherapy.org/
- American Association for Marriage and Family Therapy: http://www.aamft.org/
- American Counseling Association: http://www.counseling.org/
- American Dance Therapy Association: https://adta.org/
- American Foundation for Suicide Prevention (AFSP): https://afsp.org/our-work/research/research-videos/
- American Music Therapy Association: https://www.musictherapy.org/
- American Psychiatric Association: https://www.psychiatry.org/
- American Psychological Association: https://www.apa.org/index
- Association for Play Therapy: http://www.a4pt.org/
- Attention Deficit Disorder Association (ADDA): https://add.org/
- Brain Spotting: https://brainspotting.com/
- Bullying at Upstand: http://www.upstand.org/
- CACREP (Council for Accreditation of Counseling & Related Educational Programs): https://www.cacrep.org/

- Children's Bureau at An Office of the Administration for Children & Families: https://www.acf.hhs.gov/cb
- Elder Abuse: http://elderabuse.org/what-is-elder-abuse/
- Emotional Freedom Technique (EFT): http://www.tappingsolutionfoundation.org/howdoesitwork/
- Eye Movement Desensitization and Reprocessing (EMDR): http://www.emdr.com/
- FDA Drug page: https://www.fda.gov/Drugs/default.htm
- National Alliance on Mental Illness: https://www.nami.org/
- National Association of Social Workers: http://www.socialworkers.org/
- National Board for Certified Counselors: http://www.nbcc.org/
- National Board of Certified Counselors: https://www.nbcc.org/
- National Sexual Assault Hotline at RAINN: https://www.rainn.org/
- North American Drama Therapy Association: https://www.nadta.org/what-is-drama-therapy.html
- PCIT International: http://www.pcit.org/for-parents.html
- Psychology Today: http://www.psychologytoday.com/
- Rethinking Therapy: http://www.rethinkingtherapy.com/
- SAMHSA, Suicide Prevention Resources: https://www.samhsa.gov/prevention/suicide.aspx
- Sandplay Therapists of America: https://www.sandplay.org/
- Somatic Experiencing: https://traumahealing.org/about-us/
- Suicide: Read this first: https://metanoia.org/suicide/

- The Gottman Institute: http://www.gottman.com/
- The National Child Traumatic Stress Network: http://www.nctsn.org/interventions/parent-child-interaction-therapy
- The National Coalition Against Domestic Violence: https://ncadv.org/statistics
- The National Institute of Mental Health: https://www.nimh.nih.gov/health/topics/attention-deficit-hyperactivity-disorder-adhd/index.shtml
- To write love on her arms: https://twloha.com/

About the Author

Jenny Simon is a higher-education professional with a Doctor of Philosophy (PhD) in Transformative Learning and Change from the California Institute of Integral Studies. She has served as an experienced Adjunct Faculty member at Southwestern University, the University of Phoenix, and the University of Arizona and has nineteen years of experience teaching adult learners. Over the years, she has attained a 97 percent approval rate from her students. Dr. Simon served as the Clinical Director for an acclaimed CACREP University, where she supervised students for their Master of Science in Clinical Mental Health Counseling. Dr. Simon is a Licensed Professional Counselor (LPC) in Arizona who focuses on trauma and Eye Movement Desensitization and Reprocessing (EMDR). As an accomplished public speaker, Dr. Simon has consulted for TV segments and magazine articles about stress. Her website is Rethinking Therapy.

If this book has helped you, would you be so kind as to post a review on Amazon? Your positive review will help get this book into the hands of more people.

Made in the USA
Middletown, DE
20 September 2019